JAPAN AND THE UNITED STATES

JAPAN AND

THE UNITED STATES
EARLY ENCOUNTERS 1791–1860

BY ALFRED TAMARIN

The Macmillan Company
Collier-Macmillan Ltd., London

INTRODUCTION

In the nineteenth century, after six decades of hesitant contact, the United States and Japan collided with an impact that perhaps is not yet fully understood by either country. Two civilizations—one very new, the other very old—confronted each other, and the effects can still be felt. The aim of this work is to watch this encounter develop, to examine it from both sides of the Pacific, hoping to dispel some of the more oversimplified one-sided accounts.

In the attempt to provide a balanced view, this work relies on the actual accounts of the early visitors from the West, though these accounts are necessarily presented in excerpted form. The Japanese point of view, which has become available by recent research, is presented in more complete form so that the documents may speak for themselves.

At the time that the American fleet dropped anchor in Tokyo Bay, the crisis inside Japan was so acute and so complex that it can only be suggested. A more comprehensive history of Japan is beyond the scope of this book.

Writing about Japan for English-language readers still presents many of the puzzles that confounded the first Western visitors to that country. There were often no words in Japanese to express some of the ideas from the West. It has developed also that the English language could not provide equivalent words for many of the unique aspects of Japanese life and society. Unfortunately, in the initial atmosphere of suspicion and distrust, misinformation—particularly regarding the positions and titles of Japanese officialdom—crept into the accounts of Commodore Matthew C. Perry and Consul (later Ambassador) Townsend Harris. Some Japanese officials appear in the American documents, but cannot be traced in other sources. The author has retained the original formulations of Japanese names and titles in the excerpts quoted, but effort has been made to avoid repeating the incorrect information elsewhere. Another problem of inconsistency was created by the variations in the spellings of names and places. For example, the Ryu-kyu islands became the Lyu-kyus and, to Perry, the Lew Chews. Okinawa's port of Naha appears as Napha.

Another difficulty is created by the different styles of writing Japanese names. The traditional usage, which places the last name before the first, has been changed to the Western style: given name, family name. The Western form has been used except within direct quotations.

Western documents provided additional contradictions, particularly the impossibility of reconciling the directly opposing statements about Bayard Taylor's connection with the United States Navy while he was with Perry in Japan. Taylor writes unhesitatingly that he joined the service; Perry, followed by his editors and biographers, lists Taylor as a civilian.

In assembling the material and illustrations for this book, the author owes debts to many people both in the United States and Japan, especially:

For guidance through the complexities of Japanese social and political history: Professor Frank Baldwin, Jr., of Columbia University's East Asian Institute; Mr. Hideo Kaneko, curator of the Far Eastern Collection, Yale University Library;

and Mr. J. Rand Castile and Miss Tomie Mochizuki, respectively the educational director and librarian of the Japan Society, New York. For access to special photographs and illustrative material: Dr. Harold P. Stern, assistant director of the Freer Gallery, Washington, D.C., and Miss Emily Biederman, Museum of Fine Arts, Boston.

For the early relationships between New England and Japan: Miss Rita Steele of the Millicent Library, Fairhaven, Massachusetts; Mr. Philip Chadwick Foster Smith, curator of Maritime History, the Peabody Museum of Salem; and Mr. Richard C. Kugler, director, Whaling Museum, New Bedford.

For making my visit to Japan especially productive: the good offices of the General Consulate of Japan, New York, and the Public Affairs Department of the Foreign Ministry, Tokyo; Messrs. Shiba, Kato and Yokoh, executives of the Japan Cultural Society in Tokyo, Kyoto and Nara; Mr. Shigetaka Kaneko of the Tokyo National Museum. For the extraordinary hospitality of the land: Mr. and Mrs. K. R. Yoshida. And for a continuing contact with Japan: Miss Michiko Kaya, executive director, International Society for Educational Information, Tokyo.

While the author's aim was to present a balanced picture, the historical event, seen from the West, researched in the West, and written in the West cannot help but appear with a prevailing Western attitude. Perhaps someone like the young Japanese student Moriyuke Tanabe, part of whose letter expressing his conflicting feelings appears at the end of this work, will one day fill out the story from the other vantage point.

Alfred Tamarin

November 1969

CONTENTS

Edo Castle, from "The Scroll of the Tokaido Road"
(Historiographical Institute, Tokyo University)

JAPAN AND THE UNITED STATES

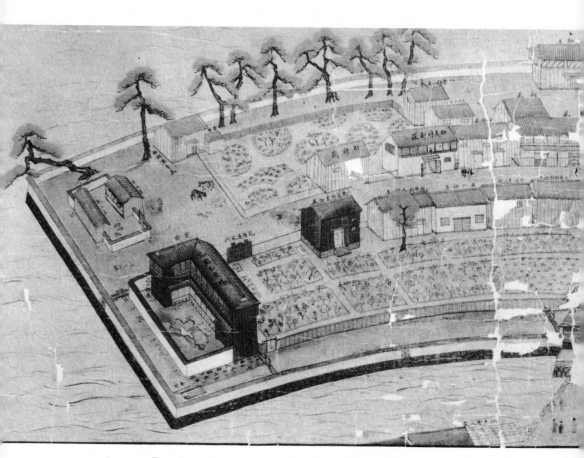

Dutch trading post on Deshima Island, Nagasaki harbor (Plan of Dutch Factory: Nagasaki Prefectural Library)

PROLOGUE

The opening of Japan is commonly associated with Commodore Matthew C. Perry, the American naval officer and diplomat who successfully negotiated the first convention, or treaty, in 1854 between the United States and Japan. Actually the process of opening Japan to the West started earlier than Commodore Perry's famous expedition and reached its climax after it—in the Treaty of Amity and Commerce concluded in 1858 by Townsend Harris. The story of the early encounters between Japan and the United States is an adventure-filled chronicle of American merchantmen and whaling ships, of shipwrecks and castaways, of a naval mission that failed as well as one that succeeded.

The story really begins in 1492 with Christopher Columbus, who was on his way to Japan when he discovered America. He was sailing west in search of the Indies and the fabled land of Jipango, as the islands of Japan had been called a century earlier by Marco Polo. Instead Columbus came upon the New World.

By the time Columbus set his course for Japan, the island empire of Nippon, as the Japanese called it, was older than any country in Europe. Its traditions dated back over two thousand years; on its throne sat the 103rd emperor of a continuous dynasty that was ten centuries old; its mythical origins went back another thousand years to the seventh century B.C.

In 1542, fifty years after Columbus' first voyage, the first Europeans reached Japan by accident. They were the Portuguese traveler and adventurer Fernám Mendes Pinto and two companions, who were aboard a Chinese pirate junk blown by a storm onto an island of Japan named Tanegashima. The Japanese were not only astonished at their first sight of Europeans, but also surprised and delighted by the

Westerners' muskets, the first firearms they had ever known, which, for many years, were called "tanegashima." By the time Mendes Pinto left five and a half months later, six hundred copies of those first guns had been made. When he returned fourteen years later, the number of weapons had grown to thirty thousand in one city alone and more than three hundred thousand were spread all over the empire.

Mendes Pinto was soon followed into Japanese waters by Portuguese trading ships, eager to fill their holds with rich cargoes of copper, camphor, lacquerware, pottery and lumber. Following the merchantmen came missionaries, zealous men of God who wanted to win the cultured, industrious people over to Christianity. Chief among them was the noted Jesuit Francis Xavier.

The Portuguese arrived in Japan in the midst of what came to be known as the "Epoch of a Warring Country." Internal warfare had been going on without interruption for eighty years and would continue for over twenty more. Old families were being wiped out. Great estates were changing hands. A new class of feudal lords, called *daimyō,* was emerging.

When the first Westerners arrived, Japan had both an emperor and a military governor called a shogun. The emperor presided ceremonially over civil and religious affairs. More effective rule was in the hands of the Shogun, or "barbarian-subduing general," who wielded the real authority in the Empire. For almost seven centuries the Japanese Imperial house had been under the dominance of a number of powerful families that acted as hereditary regents. The first of these families was the Fujiwara (857–1160). It was displaced by the Taira (1160–1185), who were succeeded by the Minamoto family (1185–1219). The Minamoto established a separate military rule (Bakufu), which was removed from the

Imperial court in Kyoto and set up four hundred miles away at Kamakura. For more than a century (1205–1333) the Kamakura Shogunate was under the influence of another important Japanese family, the Hōjō.

In 1333 the power of the Hōjō family was ended, and Imperial rule was restored for a very short time. In 1336 Takauji Ashikaga, from one of the wealthiest, most powerful houses in the eastern province, defeated the Imperial forces and established his own family as hereditary Shoguns. In the beginning of the rule of the Ashikaga, the country found itself torn by civil war, with rival emperors claiming the throne, one in Kyoto, the other in the Yoshino Mountains in the south.

Conflict between the rival lords and families, often bordering on anarchy, continued throughout the period of the Ashikaga and well into the sixteenth century. The arrival of the Portuguese added not only gunpowder but militant Christianity to the struggle.

In 1568, Oda Nobunaga, a powerful lord from central Japan, seized Kyoto, ending the reign of the Ashikaga Shogunate. Nobunaga set out to unify Japan, and one of his generals, Hideyoshi Toyotomi, conquered the western and southern provinces. Later, in 1590, Hideyoshi won the allegiance of the eastern and northern territories, completing the unification of the land. One of his prominent vassals, Ieyasu Tokugawa, set up military headquarters at Edo, which dominated the great eastern plains of Japan. Edo (also spelled Yedo or Jeddo) is known today as Tokyo.

The defeated lords looked around for new ways to recover their strength. They saw in their midst a strange new people, with formidable ships and armaments, highly profitable commerce and fierce religious convictions. In 1570 a local lord on the far western island of Kyushu opened the harbor of a minor fishing village, Nagasaki, to foreign trade. A few years later, several leading Japanese lords in the south embraced Christianity. Their example was followed by thousands, and by 1582 Japanese converts to Christianity were estimated at 150,000, served by two hundred churches.

Hideyoshi's death in 1598 led to a renewal of warfare among rival factions struggling for power. In 1600, Ieyasu defeated all opponents and established himself as ruler of the entire island empire. He had himself officially appointed Shogun and the title was made hereditary in the Tokugawa family, where it would remain for the next 264 years (1603–1867). The Emperor and his court remained in Kyoto, while the Shogun set up his military capital at Edo.

During the first years of the Tokugawa Shogunate trade with the West seemed a valuable policy. Around 1602 Spanish traders were invited to set up posts in the eastern regions to rival the Portuguese establishments in the west, but the effort proved unsuccessful. The Dutch were called in to create commercial outposts in western Japan in 1609. The English joined the trading with Japan in 1612.

The attitude of the ruling Shogun, however, began to undergo a dramatic change as he came to realize that commerce with the West could be carried on independently of religion. For centuries Japan had known almost no religious intolerance, accepting all beliefs equally. But Christianity aroused two suspicions. A Spanish sea captain had boasted that trade and religion would be followed by conquest, as they had in the Philippines. The Shogun also feared that his defeated rivals were plotting against his rule under the cover of the new religion. As a result, the second Shogun of the new Tokugawa dynasty began a campaign of persecution of Christians in Japan, whose number by 1617 was reaching over three hundred thousand. Missionaries from the West were banished or executed if they did not deny their faith. For the next two decades Christian blood in Japan was spilled freely. At the same time the Shogun was developing a policy of national isolation to keep Christian influences away from Japanese shores. In 1623 the English decided to give up their trading post in Japan. The next year the Spanish traders were expelled. In 1636 all Japanese were forbidden to leave the country and all who went abroad were to be beheaded if they returned. To make sure that no foreign travel would be possible, the law forbade the building of any ship large enough to venture beyond the shelter of the Japanese coasts.

The bloody climax of the policy of national isolation in Japan came in 1637, when thirty-seven thousand peasants on the peninsula of Shimabara, near the western port of Nagasaki, rose in revolt. For years these poor peasants had been persecuted for their Christian beliefs; then finally they rebelled, holding out for three months until their food and ammunition were gone. Every one of the rebels was slaughtered in a massacre that wiped out Christianity in Japan. An inscription was raised over the mass of dead: "So long as the sun shall warm the earth, let no Christian be so bold as to come to Japan; and let all know that the king of Spain himself, or the Christian's God, or the Great God of all, if he violates this command, shall pay for it with his head."

The Shogun suspected the Portuguese of complicity in the peasant rebellion on Shimabara, and the following year he expelled them all. Only the Dutch and some Chinese traders remained, serving for the next two hundred years as Japan's only link with the outside world.

In 1641 the Dutch traders were moved to a man-made island in the harbor at Nagasaki. They were fenced in, in almost prisonlike fashion, watched over constantly, surrounded by spies and informers, and subjected to endless humiliations and indignities. These conditions were endured for the privilege of sending a few trading ships from Batavia (now called Jakarta) on the island of Java, where the Dutch East India Company had its Far Eastern base. The number of trading voyages was finally reduced to one a year.

The artificial island, called Deshima, was described by a German physician, Dr. Engelbert Kaempfer, who was employed as the medical officer of the Dutch colony in the seventeenth century. The name Deshima, he explained, meant "advanced island," or "island before the town." It was built up at a point in the harbor where the sea was shallow and filled with sand banks and rocks. Its foundations and outer walls were built of cut stone, just high enough to keep out the sea at high tide. He described its shape as resembling "a fan without a handle."

From 1641 on, once every year, the chief Dutch agent at Deshima traveled overland to the palace of the Shogun at Edo almost eight hundred miles away. He brought with him valuable gifts for the military governor, his family and his court. Dr. Kaempfer described one such visit to Edo.

The audience with the Shogun took place in the "Hall of a Hundred Mats," where the Dutch agent "crept forwards on his hands and feet, and falling on his knees bowed his head to the ground and retired again in absolute silence, crawling exactly like a crab." Afterward the Dutch group was ordered to amuse the members of the court. "Now we had to dance, jump, represent a drunken man, speak broken Japanese, paint, read Dutch, German, sing, put on one cloak and throw them off again."

In 1775, one year before the United States declared its independence from Great Britain, another physician, Dr. Karl

Peter Thunberg, traveled to Japan aboard the annual Dutch trading ship. He reached Nagasaki harbor, where, as he described it, "the high mountains formed a roundish internal harbor in the shape of a half moon." There were several outlooks on the mountains, equipped with telescopes, so that the arrival of ships could be immediately reported to the governor of the harbor. As the ship approached its anchorage inside the harbor, it broke out a great many pennants of different colors.

Westerners in Japan; six-panel screen
(Suntory Museum of Art, Tokyo)

It sailed past two guard posts, one on either side of the port, where it fired its cannons in salute. The vessel anchored alongside the island of Deshima, not more than a musket shot from Nagasaki itself.

On the day the ship arrived, all prayer books and Bibles were collected and put into a chest which was nailed shut. The chest was turned over to the Japanese until the ship's departure to keep Christian books from entering the country.

Preparations for the arrival of the Japanese officials were begun. A carpet, protected by a canopy, was set out on the deck. A muster was prepared of the entire ship's company, numbering 144 men, including 34 slaves. Each person's name and age were given, but not his nationality since all were supposed to be Dutch. As soon as the Japanese came aboard, the muster was turned over to them and the whole crew was called up to be counted. Every morning and evening the procedure of counting the crew was repeated, so that no one could leave without the knowledge of the port officials.

Several large guard ships were stationed around the Dutch merchantman to forestall any illegal traffic, and every hour smaller boats were rowed around the anchored vessel to keep it under the closest watch.

Europeans were customarily searched as they left the ship and again before they were permitted to set foot on land. Pockets were turned inside out. Body searches were common and slaves had even the hair on their heads examined. Beds were frequently ripped open; iron spikes were thrust into the butter tubs and sweetmeat jars; holes were cut in the cheeses and thick wires used to probe into them.

On arriving, the captain dressed himself in a blue silk coat, trimmed with silver lace and cut very large, which he stuffed with a large cushion to make himself appear bulky. Dutch captains, since they were exempt from search, wore large coats of this kind to smuggle forbidden wares into Japan. With his capacious coat stuffed with hidden merchandise, the captain generally made three trips a day between the ship and the shore, frequently so loaded down that he needed two sailors to support him.

Disagreeable tidings awaited the new arrivals. Fresh orders had come that the Dutch captain was to stop wearing his large coat and submit to search along with everyone else. These orders had been issued because a Dutch ship that had been abandoned in a gale at sea had been found carrying great quantities of forbidden goods, all belonging to the captain and the chief agent. The new rules meant the loss of considerable personal profit for the Dutch captain. It was the end of the practice which for years had seen these ships' masters dressed not only in bulging overcoats but wearing large breeches also stuffed with contraband. The suddenly slender appearance of these Dutchmen astonished many of the Japanese, who had believed they were actually as fat and bulky as they appeared to be.

Over the years the Dutch had tried hundreds of tricks to sneak forbidden merchandise past the inspectors. Once a parrot, hidden in the breeches of a ship's officer, began to talk during the search. To add to these petty deceptions, the seamen from the Dutch ships sometimes showed great discourtesy to the Japanese, who in turn looked on their visitors with hatred and scorn. In Japan Westerners came to be called "barbarians."

Dr. Thunberg, however, was eager to learn as much as he could about Japan. He tried to acquire a knowledge of the language, even though it was strictly forbidden to foreigners.

For over two centuries Nagasaki was the only harbor in Japan where foreign ships were permitted to anchor: any vessel driven by wind or weather onto the coast of Japan, or in need of water or supplies, was immediately ordered there. Only the Dutch and Chinese were allowed to land and engage in trade.

The island of Deshima was also described by Dr. Thunberg. It was quite small, some 600 feet long and 125 feet broad. A bridge joined it to the mainland; at low tide it spanned only a muddy ditch. The island was enclosed on all sides by a wooden fence with only two gates: one opening toward Nagasaki, the other toward the sea. The gate to the sea was open only when a ship was loading or unloading cargo. The town gate was under constant guard and locked every night. Anyone going in or out was searched at the nearby guardhouse. Inside the walls there was another house for magistrates who constantly policed the settlement, taking notice of every occurrence and reporting to their master. The Dutch were obliged to spend almost all their time within this small confine. For the few who remained throughout the year, it was a disagreeable experience, according to Dr. Thunberg.

Early in March 1776 Thunberg set out from Nagasaki on the traditional journey to Edo to deliver the gifts of the Dutch to the Shogun and his court. The entourage consisted of three Europeans: the doctor, the chief Dutch agent and his secretary. The rest of the retinue consisted of two hundred men, mostly servants, porters, valets and interpreters.

The Westerners traveled in large, handsome sedan chairs called *norimono*—a welcome change, Dr. Thunberg wrote, from Dr. Kaempfer's trip on horseback in the cold and rain taken almost a century before. The *norimono* were made of thin board and bamboo cane, with windows in front and on either side. A long pole was fastened to the roof, by which the chair was carried on bearers' shoulders. The caravan made a splendid spectacle as it moved slowly overland from Nagasaki to Edo. Everywhere the travelers were received with princely honors and ceremonies.

On the day of the audience with the Shogun in Edo the Dutch dignitaries dressed in European style, wearing costly silks interwoven with silver and laced with gold. They arrived at the Shogun's palace and were immediately conducted into an antechamber, where they tried to sit in Japanese fashion on their knees, with their weight on their heels. But it was too tiring a position for those unaccustomed to it, and the Dutch were grateful for their long cloaks, under which they could relax and stretch their cramped legs. While they waited, numbers of people, including high officials, came in to stare, curious about everything connected with these odd Westerners. Mostly they asked for samples of writing, for which they proffered their fans.

While he was in Edo, Dr. Thunberg continued to search for material about Japan even though it was forbidden to foreigners. The sale of maps of the country and towns to strangers was punishable by death; nevertheless Thunberg managed to purchase several: a general plan of the country and detailed maps of the cities of Nagasaki, Kyoto and Edo.

A little more than half a century later, in 1828, another physician, also attached to the Dutch settlement at Deshima, was caught acquiring forbidden maps of Japan. The Japanese supplier was beheaded and the physician, Dr. P. F. von Siebold, was expelled from Japan. Von Siebold's maps were later to prove of some use to Commodore Perry when the American naval squadron sailed into the unfamiliar waters of Edo Bay.

Below: *The* Lady Washington, *drawn by Robert Haswell*
(*Massachusetts Historical Society; P: George Cushing*)

Right: *Captain James Devereux and the* Franklin (*The Peabody Museum of Salem*)

1. THE FIRST ENCOUNTERS

United States relationships with Japan began almost immediately after the American Revolution. Eight years later the first of the new Yankee ships, sailing from Atlantic Coast ports in search of trade, reached Japanese waters. Other fast clippers followed, and later American whaling ships, pursuing their profitable prey across the Pacific into the uncharted seas of Japan.

Japan had been behind its curtain of self-imposed isolation for more than a century and a half when the first American ships appeared off its coasts. During that whole time, what little was known in the West about the Japanese came exclusively from Dutch sources. The Japanese, in turn, had to rely on the Dutch for information about the rest of the world. Although the educated Japanese became surprisingly well informed about historical and scientific developments in the West, most of the Japanese people were too intimidated to want to learn much about the "barbarians." Even Japanese seamen, who might come into unexpected contact with foreign sailors, were kept in almost total ignorance of the great advances that had taken place in seamanship and navigation.

The first American ships to reach Japan were the *Lady Washington*, out of Boston, Captain Kendrick master, and the *Grace*, out of New York, Captain Douglas. The two American vessels entered a southern Japanese harbor together in 1791 with sea otter for sale. The Japanese were unfamiliar with otter fur and had no knowledge of how to use it, so no business was transacted. Six years later, the *Eliza*, also out of New York, put in an appearance at Nagasaki. On the bridge was Captain Stewart, who had replaced the Stars and Stripes with the blue, white and orange flag of the Dutch before he entered the harbor.

This substitution of flags had taken place because of the

war between England and France, in which Holland was also involved. France had overrun the Netherlands, taking over all Dutch commerce and shipping. Dutch vessels thus became enemy ships to the British and prizes of war for the British navy. The Dutch East India Company no longer dared to use its own ships from its base at Batavia to carry on the trade with Japan. Instead it chartered the vessels of a neutral nation like the United States: they were protected at sea by their own flag and raised the Dutch colors only as they approached Japan.

This situation led to the first attempt in many years to loosen the Dutch stranglehold on Japan's commercial intercourse with the West. The appearance of the *Eliza* outside the harbor at Nagasaki made the Japanese authorities very suspicious. Here was a vessel flying the Dutch flag, but all its crew spoke English. The Nagasaki authorities were dumbfounded. It took strong persuading to convince the Japanese officials that these English were not real English but a different kind of English; that they did not come from England but from another country, which was governed by a different "king" with different laws; and that the ship and its crew had nothing really to do with the trade, but were only employed by the Dutch as carriers because of the war. The magistrate of Nagasaki finally accepted the story and consented to consider the *Eliza* a Dutch ship.

The following year Captain Stewart again appeared with the *Eliza,* and there began a series of adventures and misadventures which prompted him to try to set up a trading arrangement on his own. As the *Eliza* was departing on her second voyage back to Batavia, the ship struck a rock in Nagasaki Bay and foundered. It took many weeks and long hours of negotiation with the Japanese before the ship could be raised and refloated. It may have been during this period that Captain Stewart conceived the idea of establishing commercial relations with the Japanese independently of the Dutch.

Repaired and reloaded, the *Eliza* sailed once more, but the ship was soon back in Nagasaki again. A violent storm had ripped out her mast and the ship made its way back into port to be refitted. All this occasioned so much delay that the second American ship, the *Franklin,* substituting as the Dutch ship for 1799, had not only arrived but had almost finished taking on her return cargo when Captain Stewart was finally ready to continue the voyage which should have been completed the year before.

A year later Captain Stewart was back in Nagasaki on another ship, claiming the *Eliza* had been wrecked with the total loss of its cargo. He had never reached Batavia, he said, but a friend had helped him buy and outfit the ship which he now had brought into Nagasaki. His intention was to sell the cargo and pay off his debts to the Dutch for the repairs of the *Eliza.* If he could take a cargo out, he would also have set a precedent for independent trading with the Japanese.

Unfortunately for Captain Stewart, the chief Dutch agent at Deshima doubted his story and suspected his real purpose. The Dutch trader claimed to have found some of the *Eliza's* cargo among the wares which Captain Stewart had brought with him in his new vessel. Arrangements were made to have the ship's cargo sold in the usual way and the debts outstanding to the Dutch were paid off out of the proceeds, but no cargo was obtained for the outward voyage. Instead Captain Stewart was arrested and ordered to Batavia to be tried for the loss of the *Eliza's* cargo.

The captain did not stay under detention in Batavia for very long, however. He escaped and was not heard from for a year or two. But in 1803 he once again appeared in Naga-

Foreign ship at Nagasaki; Japanese hand scroll (Honolulu Academy of Arts)

saki Bay, this time openly flying the American flag, with an avowedly American cargo, and seeking the right to trade and to supply his ship with fresh water and oil. His request to trade was flatly refused; and when his needs were supplied, he was forced to depart.

The second American ship, the *Franklin,* which the Dutch had hired for the voyage of 1799, was out of Boston, Captain James Devereux of Salem, Massachusetts, in command. The cargo to Japan consisted of cloves, cotton yarns, chintz, sugar, tin, black pepper, elephants' teeth and the year's supplies for the Dutch colony on Deshima. On its return the *Franklin* would bring copper, camphor, boxes and boards. Its charter price was to be paid in coffee, sugar, black pepper, cloves, indigo, tin, cinnamon and nutmeg.

Along with the contract for the charter, Captain Devereux was handed a letter of "Instructions on His Arrival in Japan," which explained what had to be done to comply with all the ceremonies expected by the Japanese of a Dutch vessel:

1) The ship was to fly all its colors on its entrance into Nagasaki.
2) A table, covered with a cloth, and two cushions were to be prepared on the quarterdeck for the Japanese officials who would immediately come on board.
3) A list was to be made of all persons on the ship, giving their stations and ages.
4) All books, particularly religious books, were to be put into a cask or chest and sealed.
5) All money was to be taken up from everyone on board and kept until after the ship's departure. This would not cause

Ship flying Dutch flags and firing a salute in Nagasaki harbor, 1802; fan-shaped Deshima at lower right (The Peabody Museum of Salem)

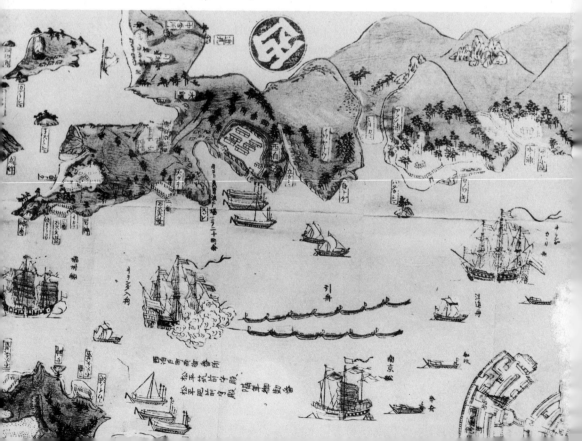

any inconvenience since nothing in Japan could be bought for cash, but only through trade, which could only be carried on by the Captain.

6) When the ship came within sight of Japan, the American colors were to be replaced by the Dutch flag, flying in the proper place, as though the ship were Dutch.

7) When the Cavalles (unidentified) appeared on the ship's starboard side and the island of Japan on its larboard side, the ship was to salute the guards on the Cavalles with nine guns.

8) As the ship passed Papenburg (an island in Nagasaki harbor), it was to fire a salute of nine guns.

9) The guardposts of the Emperor and the Empress, which would appear on the starboard and larboard sides at the same time, were to be saluted with seven and nine guns respectively, the first all starboard guns, the second all larboard.

10) Advancing next into the roads of Nagasaki and anchoring, the ship was to fire a salute of thirteen guns.

11) The Japanese commissioner was to be saluted with nine guns when he first came aboard. At the same time some colors were to be hoisted in his honor. It did not matter what the colors were as long as they were not Spanish or Portuguese. But at all times the Dutch colors were to be in their proper place.

12) When the Japanese official left for shore, his departure was to be accompanied by a salute of nine guns.

13) Whenever a salute was about to be fired, great care was to be taken to alert all the surrounding boats to prevent anyone from being hurt.

14) Once the ship had been anchored and the harbor saluted, the muster of the ship's personnel would be examined and checked by an actual count of the people on board. All arms

and ammunition were to be sent ashore until the ship's departure, when the material would be returned.

15) If any other ceremonies were forgotten, the agents of the company at Nagasaki would be on hand to give the missing instructions.

In 1800, the third American ship to carry the annual Dutch cargo to Japan was the *Massachusetts,* Captain William V. Hutchings, master. On board as captain's clerk was William Cleveland, a young member of a seagoing family from Salem, who wrote a journal of the voyage. The *Massachusetts,* like the *Franklin,* flew all the flags and fired all the salutes required by the elaborate ceremonial procedures.

Mr. Cleveland's first impressions of Japan were enthusiastic, even though he had been quite ready at first to believe that the Japanese were as haughty and reserved as the Dutch had described them.

Among the first visitors to come aboard was the enterprising Captain Stewart, who at that time was in Nagasaki with his new ship, having reported the *Eliza* lost. A representative of the magistrate of Nagasaki had come aboard and gone directly to the carpet spread for him on the deck. He remained there under the canopy and all visitors to the ship and all lesser Japanese officials went over to pay their respects with a very low bow. Even the chief Dutch trader bowed so low that Cleveland thought he was perhaps renouncing his religion, not merely doing honor to a government official. As was the custom, a Japanese guard boat was stationed a short distance from the *Massachusetts.*

Two days later the entire ship's company passed muster before the Japanese magistrate and a count was taken. Persons not well enough to come above deck were checked below.

When all hands were accounted for, the business of unloading the ship's cargo began. Boats started to take some of the passengers' stores ashore, as well as livestock such as sheep, goats, poultry and even an orangutan. Every boatload was accompanied by an inspector to prevent the ship's crew from pilfering. The crew were searched as they left the ship, as they stepped ashore and as they returned to the boats.

Captain Stewart regaled his countrymen with tales of smugglers and smuggling and warned the Americans of bloody penalties if they were caught. Just a few nights previous, he told the men on the *Massachusetts,* the captain and crew of a Chinese junk had been captured in a smuggling attempt and would all probably be beheaded. The visiting captain told them about Japanese hostility to Christianity and described a plaque with a figure of Christ which had been placed in a public square to be trampled upon. Some Japanese even drew blood from their fingers to smear the image, inflicting what was considered the highest insult.

During the course of the vessel's stay Cleveland changed his opinions about the Japanese. He found many eager to learn English. Some already spoke Dutch. He found them quick to understand and easy to make contact with. They proved respectful and engaging to the Americans, most of whom grew extremely pleased with them, despite the strong prejudices the Dutch had tried to foster. The youthful captain's clerk found that the stories of Japanese cruelty were exaggerated and often entirely unfounded.

It was astonishing to Cleveland, too, to find what a low opinion the Japanese had of America. Some believed that the whole country was not as big as the town of Nagasaki. They were confounded by a map of the world, showing how much larger America was than all the Dutch domains. It was apparent that the Dutch had spread exaggerated tales to make the Japanese think their country the biggest in the West.

The crew of the *Massachusetts* had very few opportunities of seeing anything of Japan or learning much about its people. From the decks buildings could be seen lit up at night, but no one could tell whether or not these were places of worship. Cleveland wondered about the religious practices of the Japanese; he heard that there were as many as three hundred temples in the city, where worshipers pulled off their shoes before entering. The first and fifteenth days of the months were supposed to be days of rest, but he could detect no distinction between them and any other day. He was curious to find out the qualifications of Japanese magistrates, but all he could learn was that they came from the highest-ranking families.

In late September one of the ship's crew died of fever. The body was placed in a wooden coffin and carried ashore, but the shipmates were not allowed to accompany it beyond the bridge connecting Deshima and the mainland. There, to Cleveland's horror, the coffin was opened and searched to make sure nothing was being smuggled into the city.

One day the Nagasaki magistrate himself came aboard to inspect the ship. His visit was ceremonious, marked by much bowing, which was required even of the captain. Servants wiped the ship's gunwales before the magistrate touched them. Tables, linens and towels were brought out from shore. The tables were set with dainties, sweetmeats, cakes and liquors, which were also carried out for him. The magistrate wanted to look over the gundeck, which was immediately cleared. He expressed a wish to see the ship's Negro cook, who was ordered on deck to give the Japanese his first sight of a black man.

After the *Massachusetts* had been in Nagasaki awhile, the crew managed to engage in small trading for lacquer boxes and fans. The complicated business procedures were annoying to the easy-going Americans, eager to make their voyage as profitable as possible.

The fifth day of the eleventh month, the traditional day of departure arrived and the ship was busily prepared to take its leave. Last-minute searches were carried out, even the compartments in the ship's writing desks were opened for inspection. Around noon, the crew aboard, the ship was unmoored and escorted from the inner harbor. For a few weeks longer, the American ship rode at anchor off Papenburg in the lower bay of Nagasaki. Dutch officials continued to visit the ship and to entertain the Americans with stories about Japan. The confusion about the country's double sovereignty is evident in Cleveland's journal entry for November 19, 1800.

"Mr. Gunniman [the Dutch agent] observed that no person, not even the Emperor himself can be permitted to go on board the ship until the [magistrates] are on board; that the Governors are not permitted to leave their habitations except at certain times and on particular occasions. The Emperor [referring to the Shogun] is permitted to pass the walls of Jeddo [Tokyo] only when called to pay his respects to the Diary [the Emperor] or Religious Emperor at Meacco [Kyoto]. The present Emperor [Shogun] has refused to visit the Diary according to the customs of the country, and this may be a step towards shaking off the yoke, as some princes of Europe have of the Pope. The Diary is acknowledged the first person in the country by the best information I can get. His power is something similar to that of the Pope of Rome formerly. His residence is at Meacco, a city of great extent and significance."

Cleveland's prediction was sixty-eight years too early and reversed. It was the Emperor who destroyed the power of the Shogun in the Meiji Restoration of 1868.

William Cleveland's brother, George, followed him to Japan in the *Margaret*, Captain Samuel Derby, the American ship chartered ain 1801 to make the passage from Batavia. George was also the captain's clerk and he, too, wrote an account of his journey.

The cargo to Japan consisted of a great variety of articles that had been the staples of the Dutch commerce for nearly two centuries: sugar, spices, sapanwood, sandalwood, rattans, glassware, cloth, medicines, all set out according to time-honored rules. On the customary day, June 20, the *Margaret* weighed anchor and set its course north. The American ship entered the harbor of Nagasaki almost a month later, flying twenty different colors. It went through the required ceremonies and fired all the necessary salutes.

George Cleveland described the intricate trading procedures which he had to go through in Nagasaki:

"Captain Derby, Mr. West (second mate) and myself carried several articles of merchandise on our own account. This has always been allowed to Dutch captains, but the sale of these articles must be made by the Japanese government. All these articles were landed on the island [Deshima], opened and displayed in a warehouse and on certain days the (Japanese) merchants were allowed to go on the island to examine them. Nothing could exceed the minuteness with which they examined everything. Among other articles we had a quantity of tumblers and wine glasses; these they measured with the greatest care, running their fingers over every part to determine what irregularities there were on the surface, and then holding each piece up to the light to see the color. They also made drawings of the different descriptions of the pieces.

"After this investigation they marked on their memorandums the number of the lot and the results of their investiga-

Ships in Nagasaki harbor, 1799;
scroll by Shiba Kokan (The Peabody Museum of Salem)

Ao. 1779.

Nagasaki.

tions. Everything we had to sell went through a similar ordeal so that to us, who were lookers on and owners of the property, nothing could be more tedious. After the goods had been sufficiently examined, a day was appointed for a sale, in the city of Nangasacca [Nagasaki] and was conducted with the greatest fairness. Captain Derby and myself went into the city attended by the requisite number of officers and proceeded to what the Dutch call the Geltchamber where we found one or more of the Upper Banyos [magistrates] seated in their usual state, and a general attendance of merchants. We were placed where we could see all that was going on and received such explanations as were requisite to an understanding of the whole business. The goods being disposed of, we were escorted back to the island with much formality, not however, until a day had been appointed by the great men for the delivery of the goods.

"No person in this country [the United States], who had not traded with people who have so little intercourse with the world, can have an idea of the trouble we had in delivering [the merchandise], which would not have been an hour's work in Salem."

The Japanese wares that were being exchanged for the ship's cargo now began arriving at shipside. The goods were brought in from the interior many hundreds of miles away and consisted of the most beautiful lacquerware, tea caddies, knife boxes, tables and the like. All were packed neatly in wooden boxes that in most other countries would have been considered fine cabinetwork. The *Margaret* also took back a great variety of porcelains and housebrooms of superior quality.

For the next eight years, with some interruptions while the war between England and French-held Holland continued, American ships carried the usual cargoes between Nagasaki and Batavia, under charter to the Dutch East India Company.

In 1811 the British attacked Batavia and the Dutch governor surrendered Java and all its dependencies, which supposedly included the Dutch trading post on Deshima. Two English ships stood off the entrance to the Japanese port in 1813, looking very much like two more American charter ships to the local authorities. It was not until they had gone through all the formalities and anchored in the inner harbor, their arms and ammunition handed over to the Nagasaki officials, that the true situation was revealed. The Dutch agent stubbornly refused to accept the news of Batavia's surrender. He would not acknowledge the authority of England. The Japanese magistrate of Nagasaki was also appalled by these fantastic events, happening so far away, which upset procedures that had existed for centuries. Contrary to their own law, the Japanese had permitted a Western trading vessel that was not Dutch into the inner harbor. There was always the possibility of bloodshed if the English decided to put up a fight. Another fiction had to be invented: the English ships became "American" vessels in the service of the Dutch.

The state of war between the English and the Dutch ended in 1814, when the French emperor Napoleon Bonaparte and his armies were driven out of the Netherlands. The Dutch were restored to their homeland in Europe and could look forward to getting back their colonial possessions in Asia. In 1817 the Dutch resumed their annual voyages to Japan in their own ships.

Inside Japan, behind its tightly shut ports, statesmen and scholars were disturbed by these events on the other side of the world. They feared that the policy of national isolation which had kept Japan at peace for almost two centuries was being threatened. More and more ships from the West were appearing off the Japanese coast. Sometimes shipwrecked crews managed to reach safety on Japanese soil, and their unwelcome presence added to the uneasiness. Japanese writers began to urge that the country strengthen its defenses to meet the "invasion" by the barbarian. In 1825, Seishizai Aizawa, a Japanese scholar, offered a series of suggestions which he called "New Proposals."

"Our Divine Land is where the sun rises and where the primordial energy originates. The heirs of the Great Sun have occupied the Imperial Throne from generation to generation without change from time immemorial. Japan's position at the head of the earth makes it the standard for the nations of the world. Indeed, it casts its light over the world, and the distance, which the resplendent imperial influence reaches, knows no limit.

"Today, the alien barbarians of the West, the lowly organs of the legs and feet of the world, are dashing about across the seas, trampling other countries underfoot, and daring, with their squinting eyes and limping feet, to override the noble nations. What manner of arrogance is this!

"The various countries of the West correspond to the feet and legs of the body. That is why their ships come from afar to visit Japan. As for the land amidst the seas which the Western barbarians call America, it occupies the hindmost region of the earth; thus, its people are stupid and simple, and are incapable of doing things. These are all according to the dispensations of nature. Thus, it stands to reason that the Westerners, by committing errors and overstepping their bounds, are inviting their own eventual downfall. But . . . unless great men appear who rally to the assistance of Heaven, the whole natural order will fall victim to the predatory barbarians, and that will be all. In the 'Art of War' it says: 'Do not depend on their not invading your land, rely on your own defense to forestall their invasion.'

"Some say that the Westerners are merely foreign barbarians, that their ships are trading vessels or fishing vessels, and that they are not people who would cause serious trouble or great harm. Such people are relying on the enemy not coming and invading their land. They rely on others, not upon themselves. If I ask such people about the state of their preparedness, about their ability to forestall an invasion, they stare blankly at me and know not what to say. How can we ever expect them to help save the natural order from subversion at the hands of the Western barbarians?"

In another section, which he called "The Dangers from the West," the same writer added:

"Now we must cope with the foreigners of the West, where

George Washington, a Japanese conception (Harold P. Stern Collection, Washington, D.C.)

every country upholds the law of Jesus and attempts there-
with to subdue other countries. Everywhere they go they set
fire to shrines and temples, deceive and delude the people, and
then invade and seize the country. Their purpose is not realized until the ruler of the land is made a subject and the people of the land subservient. As they have gained momentum,
they have attempted to foist themselves on our Divine Land,
as they have already done in Luzon [the Philippines] and
Java.

"Recently, there has appeared what is known as Dutch
Studies, which had its inception among our official interpreters [at Nagasaki]. It has been concerned primarily with
the reading and writing of Dutch, and there is nothing harmful about it. However, these students, who make a living by
passing on whatever they hear, have been taken in by the
vaunted theories of the Western foreigners. They enthusiasti-
cally extol these theories, some going so far as to publish books
about them in the hope of transforming our civilized way of
life into that of the barbarians. And the weakness of some for
novel gadgets and rare medicines, which delight the eye and
enthrall the heart, have led many to admire foreign ways. If
someday the treacherous foreigner should take advantage of
this situation and lure ignorant people to his ways, our people
will adopt such practices as eating dogs and sheep and wearing woolen clothing. And no one will be able to stop it. We
must not permit the frost to turn to hard ice. We must become fully aware of its harmful and weakening effect and
make an effort to check it. Now the Western foreigners,
spurred by the desire to wreak havoc upon us, are daily prying
into our territorial waters. And within our own domain evil
teachings flourish in a hundred subtle ways. It is like nurturing
barbarians within our own country."

Still the American ships, braving the fierce gales of the Japan seas, came on, their chance meetings with Japanese boats the most frequent contact between the two peoples for thirty years. The same fierce storms sometimes blew the small Japanese vessels out to sea into the Japan Current, which sweeps from the eastern shores of Japan in a large semicircle that washes the western coasts of Canada and the United States. Several of these shipwrecked Japanese sailors were picked up in Canada in the 1830s and a mission organized to return them to their homeland. C. W. King, an American merchant, chartered the *Morrison,* a powerful, fast-sailing vessel, to bring seven of the Japanese castaways back to their home. To show his peaceful intentions, he removed all the ship's cannon and carried as passengers his wife and three Christian missionaries. One was S. Wells Williams, who would accompany Commodore Perry as an interpreter sixteen years later.

King's account of his voyage was the first book about Japan to be published in America. The journey began in China early in July 1837, and the shores of Japan were sighted late the same month. The *Morrison* was headed for the port of Uraga, ten or twelve miles below Edo. It was just two miles from its intended anchorage when it was fired upon by the cannon of a low white fortress overlooking the port. The ship immediately veered toward shore and dropped anchor. Its sails were furled and every effort made to show that the vessel was not hostile and that it had no intention of forcing its way up the bay to Edo.

Soon twenty boats or so brought out several hundred Japanese, who were welcomed on board the unarmed ship. Presents were distributed, consisting mostly of brightly colored cloth, shining American five-cent pieces, sweet wine and biscuits. Through all these occurrences the shipwrecked sailors stayed below deck, out of sight of their countrymen.

Just before dawn the next day, however, a battery of two to four guns opened fire on the vessel, which lay with her rudder exposed. It was evident at once that the bombardment was in earnest. The shot from one or two of the guns fell considerably short, but ball after ball from the heavier pieces passed directly overhead. It was imperative to get the ship out of range without losing a moment. The windlass was manned and the sails loosed; it was thought that if the firing was just to drive off the *Morrison,* the activity on shipboard would have been proof enough of its preparations to depart. But evidently the Japanese intentions were more lethal. The firing continued for the entire half hour that it took to get under way. It kept up as the ship sailed off, falling harmlessly in the *Morrison*'s wake until it was clearly out of danger. Only one ball struck the ship, inflicting minor damage and no injuries. But it was clear that only the absence of a telescope or bad marksmanship had saved the Americans from serious harm.

The *Morrison* headed out of the bay which it had entered the day before with such anticipation. The shipwrecked Japanese begged not to be put ashore in a territory where such a deadly reception was possible, so the ship headed for another port, Kagoshima. It was again greeted with artillery.

King had little doubt that news of the *Morrison*'s arrival had been rushed to the capital at Edo. He found it hard to believe that orders had been returned in the few hours since he was first sighted, because if that were the case, he wrote, "we were fired on as *unarmed, friendly Americans* and that under imperial sanction." He leaned to the idea that the local officials had been acting under general orders not directed particularly against the ship's American colors.

人島東面之圖

船中ヨリ鳥ノ
大ニ此ニ群聚スル
時ヲ望ミニ其甚シ
キハ殆ント山形ヲ
失フ事アリト云

John Mung

In the early 1840s a fourteen-year-old Japanese castaway was rescued by a New England sea captain and brought to the United States, where he was taught English, barrel-making and Western navigation. Called Johnny Mung by the Yankee sailors, he came to be known as Manjiro Nakahama in Japan. Illustration from Nakahama's account of his adventures   (The Millicent Library, Fairhaven, Mass.)

The mission a failure, King returned to China.

Almost ten years later, in 1846, the United States Government decided that something had to be done officially. More sailors were being shipwrecked on Japanese coasts and coming home with hair-raising tales of brutality and imprisonment. American commerce was expanding as steam power was being developed and new steam-driven vessels were being put into service, crossing the ocean in days rather than months. Two armed vessels of the United States Navy, the *Columbus* and the *Vincennes,* under the command of Commodore James Biddle, were ordered to Japan to negotiate some kind of understanding with the isolated island empire. Biddle arrived safely in the great bay of Edo and began a series of conferences with the Japanese.

While the Commodore was in the midst of his negotiations, unbeknownst to him, seven American sailors, survivors of the crew of the whaler *Lawrence,* Captain Baker, out of Poughkeepsie, New York, were being held in prison inside Japan.

One incident that had unpleasant repercussions for years afterward happened as Commodore Biddle was about to go on board a Japanese ship anchored in Edo Bay. The American naval commander had been persuaded to accept the reply to his letter from the President of the United States on board a Japanese vessel, since the President's letter had been delivered on an American ship. The Commodore described the singular event himself:

"I went alongside the junk in the ship's boat in my uniform. At the moment that I was stepping on board, a Japanese on the deck of the junk gave me a blow or a push, which threw me back in the boat."

Biddle was outraged and might have reacted with gunfire, but he had strict instructions to maintain peaceable contact with the Japanese at all costs. He was assured that the man responsible would be dealt with severely and the matter was dropped, with nothing further demanded in reparation or apology.

Ten days after his arrival in Edo Bay, Commodore Biddle was handed an unsigned note, which read:

"The object of this communication is to explain the reason why we refuse to trade with foreigners who come to this country across the sea for that purpose.

"This has been the habit of our nation from time immemorial. In all cases of a similar kind that have occurred, we have positively refused to trade. Foreigners have come to us from various quarters, but have always been received in the same way. In taking this course with regard to you, we only pursue our accustomed policy. We can make no distinction between foreign nations—we treat them all alike; and you, as Americans, must receive the same answer with the rest. It will be of no use to renew the attempt, as all applications of the kind, however numerous they may be, will steadily be rejected.

"We are aware that our customs are in this respect different from those of some other countries, but every nation has a right to manage its affairs in its own way.

"The trade carried on with the Dutch at Nagasaki is not to be regarded as furnishing a precedent for trade with other foreign nations. The place is one of few inhabitants and very little business is transacted, and the whole affair is of no importance.

"In conclusion, we have to say that the Emperor positively refuses the permission you desire. He earnestly advises you to depart immediately, and to consult your own safety by not appearing again upon our coast."

Commodore Biddle, after receiving the note, weighed anchor and sailed away.

The mission was even more harmful than a simple failure. For years the memory remained of the insulted American who would not fight. The dignity of America in the minds of the Japanese was lowered. Imprisoned seamen who threatened the Japanese with retribution by the U. S. Navy were laughed

U. S. SLOOP OF WAR VINCENNES.

Ship of Commodore Biddle's expedition, 1846;
lithograph by N. Currier (P: United States Navy)

at. Even in Western seafaring circles Commodore Biddle's
mission elicited some derision. A publication for sailors in
Honolulu, the *Seaman's Friend,* commented in 1848:

"There is a growing conviction throughout the civilized
world that the time is rapidly approaching when the exclusive
policy of the Japanese will be done away with, and a commercial intercourse be opened between that and other nations
of the earth besides the Dutch. Occasionally rumor reaches us
that the British East India Squadron is hovering upon the
coast of Japan, but no sooner have we begun to credit the report than we learn that is a mere rumor. The report flies
around the world that an American commodore, on board a
'line of battleship,' is bound for Japan. Now something will
be done. The stately vessel anchors near Jeddo [Tokyo]. Communication is attempted with the Japanese authorities. The
emperor sends word to supply the 'big junk' with what she

wanted, up anchor, be off and never return. All this was done in the most genteel and civil style, and what could a gallant commodore do? He had fought the British, but he must not fight the Japanese."

The mystery behind Japan's closed gates appealed strongly to adventurous minds in the West. In 1848 a young American named Ranald MacDonald decided to try opening the gates single-handed. He first heard of Japan from the news of the rescue of the shipwrecked Japanese seamen whom C. W. King later tried to return home in the *Morrison*.

MacDonald's story has since appeared in his own autobiography, but that year its beginning was printed in *Seaman's Friend* in Honolulu:

"After remaining in the vessel [the *Plymouth*, out of Sag Harbor, New York], in the fall of 1847, he [Ranald Mac-Donald] requested his discharge unless Captain Edwards would consent to leave him the next season somewhere upon the coast of Japan. Young MacDonald is a son of Archibald MacDonald, Esq., formerly of the Hudson's Bay Company, Columbia. This young man received a good education, but instead of pursuing a mercantile life on shore, betook himself to sea. Soon after the *Plymouth* left Lahaina [in Hawaii], he began to make arrangements for penetrating the hermetically sealed empire of Japan. Captain Edwards allowed him to make choice of the best boat belonging to the ship. The carpenter decked her over. Having gathered his all together, he embarked upon his perilous and adventurous enterprise."

No more was heard from Ranald MacDonald that year. A ship, the *Uncas*, cruising nearby, reported that she had picked up the rudder of his tiny craft. Whether the small boat ever reached shore or was swamped in the surf no one yet knew.

The daring twenty-four-year-old sailor steered his boat for a bay in an island which he sighted in the distance. He found the island uninhabited so he tried a preplanned experiment: he capsized the boat and righted it again, a maneuver which would enable him to pretend to be the survivor of a shipwreck. He stayed on the deserted island for two nights so that the *Plymouth* would be still farther away. On the third day he headed for a Japanese island ten miles distant. Halfway there he overturned his boat, let everything but his chest float off, abandoned his rudder and then, righting the vessel, set it drifting toward land. That night he spent on the sea. Early the next morning he was spied by some of the Japanese inhabitants, who launched a boat and approached him timidly. MacDonald jumped into their boat, tied his own to it and made signs that he would like to go ashore.

On land MacDonald was treated kindly, but after a few days officers from the capital of the province arrived and put him behind bars. On July 28, 1848—the twenty-second day of the sixth moon, according to the Japanese calendar—the magistrate of the district of Matsumae on the island of Hokkaido, sent a report to the Shogun's government:

"On the 2nd inst. about the hour of ape [4:00 P.M.] a foreigner was driven in a boat to the shore of Notsuka in Rishiri Island in my domain of Western Yezo [now Hokkaido]. As he had wet clothes on and seemed very tired, he was immediately taken to the guard-house at Notsuka and given food, etc. On being informed of the event, some of my retainers at the Guards station of Soya went to Notsuka and tried to get information [from the foreigner]. As, however, they could not understand each other, the questions were put by signs and the foreigner also answered by signs, so that the precise facts could not be ascertained, but he was understood to say that he left the mothership alone in the boat and after some time the wind and the sea, getting high, his boat capsized twice; that his compass dropped into the sea and he was drifting aimlessly when he saw a high mountain and rowing towards it landed on the shore. As the boat had suffered no damage he was told by signs to sail home, but he seemed to hesitate to go out into the wide sea in that small boat. He was therefore told by signs that he would be allowed to stay and as he nodded assent he was taken to the Guards station of Soya and was well treated and escorted. The preceding is the report of my retainers at the station. I inform you of the above and wish to know what is to be done with this foreigner."

The Shogun's government sent back its instructions on August 17: "The drifted foreigner mentioned in your letter should be first taken to Esashi and forwarded to Nagasaki at the earliest convenience."

The young Westerner did not find life too unpleasant in his Japanese prison. He was regaled with sweetmeats and, according to his own testimony, treated with kindness. He learned that he had been preceded by fifteen American mutineers from the whaler *Lagoda,* who had made several attempts to escape. One of the imprisoned Americans had left behind a rough spoon which was turned over to MacDonald. On October 1 he was put aboard another ship for Nagasaki, arriving there a fortnight later. After remaining on the boat for two additional days, he was landed on October 17 and taken to a small enclosure next to the town hall. There an interpreter, Enosuke Moriyama, met him and told him that in front of the first door of the town hall he would see a sculptured image on the ground, which was described as "the devil of Japan" and which he was to step on. MacDonald put his foot on the plaque but could not see it too clearly, he said, because of the crowd which pushed him forward. It was a metallic plate about a foot in diameter, on which he could make out a representation of the Virgin Mary and the Infant Christ.

Inside the town hall MacDonald was requested to sit down in Japanese fashion, kneeling on a mat. He tried one foot at a time and managed to get down on both knees. Soon the Magistrate came in and MacDonald was told that he must bow low to make a "compliment" to him. MacDonald did as he was told. The Japanese began interrogating him. They asked his name, his birthplace, the port from which he had sailed and his residence. MacDonald replied that he hailed from Oregon,

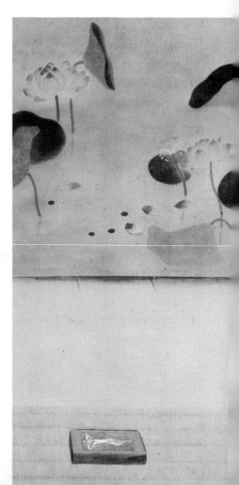

Ceremony of treading on a Christian religious image; painting by Kobayashi Kokei (Tokyo National Museum)

New York and Canada, hoping that either an American or an English vessel might arrive and liberate him. He was asked about his ship, his reasons for leaving it and finally about his religious beliefs. He answered, he said, that he believed in a God in Heaven; in the Father, Son and Holy Ghost; and in the Lord and Savior, Jesus Christ. He was then taken from the town hall and put into a prison, where he remained until April 1849.

MacDonald's arrival at Nagasaki was duly noted in the official records: "Ranarudo Makudonaruto, fisherman of Canada, 24 years old, has been received in charge. He said that there was no god nor Buddha. He cultivated his heart and will and worshipped heaven in order to get clear understand-

ing and enjoy happiness. He has nothing else to repeat."

About April 17, signal guns were fired in Nagasaki harbor. MacDonald knew that these meant the approach of a ship, but of what flag he could not tell. The guns also called in troops from the neighboring towns and districts, swelling the town's normal garrison of 650 to over 6,000. Something extraordinary was in the wind: the arrival of an American warship, the *Preble,* under Commander James Glynn. MacDonald was brought to the Dutch colony at Deshima, where he was made comfortable until he was turned over to the U.S. Navy.

During his imprisonment several of the Japanese interpreters came to MacDonald to learn English, a fact which probably served to insure him better treatment than otherwise. One, Moriyama, became the official interpreter for the Japanese commissioners dealing with Commodore Perry five years later.

Word of the imprisonment of the fifteen crewmen of the *Lagoda* had reached the United States East Indian squadron and the *Preble* had been dispatched to obtain their freedom. At first the Japanese tried to warn off the American commander, but he pushed on determinedly and anchored off the town of Nagasaki, where the seamen were being confined. News of the ship's arrival was kept from the Americans at first. They had warned their Japanese captors that a man-of-war would come for them, but the Japanese, remembering the unavenged insult to Commodore Biddle three years earlier, had laughed contemptuously. Now the United States warship had appeared and there was great excitement in Nagasaki. On the morning of April 26, the interpreter came to MacDonald's prison and showed him a letter in English reported to be an order to the *Preble* to leave Nagasaki as soon as the fifteen prisoners were turned over. The interpreter needed MacDonald's advice as to the relative rank of the ship's captain, counted in the order of succession from the highest chief in the United States down. MacDonald listed the President, the Secretary of the Navy, Commodore and Commander. Glynn's rank seemed high enough to excite the surprise of the Japanese.

The *Seaman's Friend* in Honolulu, reporting the rescue of MacDonald and the crew of the *Lagoda,* added:

"During their captivity these young men gathered much interesting information respecting the country and Japanese government. MacDonald, but more especially [Robert] McCoy [of the *Lagoda*], succeeded in acquiring a tolerable knowledge of the colloquial Japanese language. We hope that ere long a more full report of these young men will be spread before the world, together with the visit of *Preble*. It opens a new chapter in the intercourse of foreigners with the exclusive Japanese."

In one of its earlier comments on the West's attempts to open Japan, the *Seaman's Friend* had said:

"While the great commercial and naval nations of the world are meditating upon some great expedition, our numerous whale ships are really doing something in the way of opening intercourse with Japan. During the last season for ships to cruise in the Japan sea [1847–48], not scores, but hundreds of vessels spread their canvas within full view of the coast. Several whale ships have fallen in with junks, exchanged civilities with them and in some instances relieved those in distress."

Japanese seamen "in distress," cast adrift on the Japan Current and swept out into the Pacific Ocean, were sometimes more terrified of being rescued than of the wind and the sea. The Japanese knew that their old laws of national isolation decreed their deaths if they returned to Japan, but they were unsure that their "barbarian" saviors would not eat

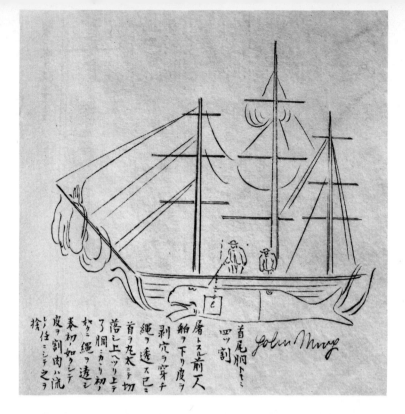

A Japanese view of an American whaling ship, from Manjiro Nakahama's account of his rescue. Nakahama returned to Japan in 1851. (The Millicent Library, Fairhaven, Mass.)

them then and there. In Japan knowledge of America was garbled by the stories spread by the Dutch. Japanese sailors knew very little about ocean-going navigation and were generally unfamiliar with the latest techniques and instruments. Their puzzlement was often comic as well as tragic.

A story of castaway Japanese mariners was written by one of a rescued crew, who was to become an American citizen with the name of Joseph Heco. Heco was born in 1837, the year that the American ship *Morrison* was driven by gunfire out of two Japanese ports, in a village on the shore of Japan's Inland Sea. His older brother and stepfather were sailors and his uncle was the captain of a large ship trading between Osaka and Edo. Heco dreamed of traveling, too, but he had little thought of seeing anything beyond his own country; indeed he did not even know of the existence of other lands and other people, or if he did, "it was to pity the barbarian who came each year or so to Nagasaki."

One day when Joseph was thirteen years old, his stepfather consented to take him on a voyage to Edo. In the ninth moon (toward the latter part of 1850) they set sail with a cargo of sake (rice wine), among other articles. The vessel was one of the largest boats of the day, about 238 tons. When the weather turned rainy and the winds became contrary, the ship put into port, where it remained for a few days, waiting for a fair wind and clear sailing. While it was there, another, newer boat arrived, also bound for Edo. Its captain invited the youngster to sail on his vessel, to which Joseph's stepfather reluctantly agreed.

At Edo, Joseph saw the forerunner of modern Tokyo; halfway through the nineteenth century there was absolutely no trace of any foreigners in the Shogun's capital; no kerosene oil lamps were on sale, no railways, tramcars, European carriages or Western costumes were to be seen as they were forty years later when Heco's book was published. But Edo in 1850 was a large and magnificent city. The visitors covered the vast distances inside the city on foot. The other means of transportation—sedan chairs or horseback—were too expensive for poor provincial sailors.

On the twentieth of the tenth moon Heco started for home. On the way down Edo Bay, he saw Uraga, where all ships entering the bay were stopped for inspection. It was off Uraga that C. W. King and the *Morrison* had been fired on in 1837 and that the American expedition under Commodore Biddle had anchored in 1846 for its conferences with the Japanese.

"The Biddle expedition caused great excitement among the nobles and officers of the government," wrote Heco. "My stepfather's junk happened to be in the harbor at the time and was pressed for service by the native authorities as one of the several hundred guard-boats which surrounded the strangers.

"While I was at home I often heard my father tell the story and speak of the fear he felt at encountering the strange visitors. The expedition remained ten days. No one was allowed to land, and the answer to the President's letter consisted of the simple sentence: *No trade can be permitted with any other country than Holland.*"

Heco and his shipmates remained at Uraga until the ship's cargo was completed. The first few days out the wind was contrary and the boat made little headway. Toward the end of the tenth moon the wind turned fair and the ship scudded along, all sails set and the yards neatly squared. The weather had every appearance of continuing favorable, so instead of stopping overnight, the ship stood its course. But in the evening a rain started and the wind suddenly increased until it was blowing a gale. The storm grew worse, the seas rose higher and the boat shook from stem to stern as it plunged down into the troughs of the waves.

In the morning the rain stopped and the wind eased off, but the sea continued high. The crew had all it could do to keep the vesssel afloat, and for moments it almost failed to do that. Without a stitch of canvas, the ship drove along at three to four knots an hour. By noon part of the cargo of barley and peas had to be thrown overboard to lighten the vessel and keep the mast from pitching out; by afternoon, it was impossible to keep the mast; and by nightfall, it was cut away. That night it became almost dead calm. The sky was filled with stars and the sea was smooth, as if nothing had happened. Only the unfortunate craft, its sail torn and flapping, its mast gone, reminded the crew of the peril that had just passed. Joseph went forward, washed his hands, rinsed out his mouth and gave thanks to the gods for his deliverance. There was always a little shrine on board a Japanese boat, in the cabin just behind the mast.

On the twenty-first day of the twelfth moon, fifty-five days after they had left Uraga, the morning broke clear and beautiful. Before the sun was up, one of the men rose early to wash and pray, when suddenly he observed directly ahead of the vessel something white, looking like a rock with a snow-capped summit. He rushed down to the cabin shouting that the ship was drifting onto an island straight ahead.

It was neither an island nor a rock, but a large vessel with tall masts and white sails. The Japanese sailors made signals with old clothes fastened to bamboo poles and the vessel responded, turned her prow toward the north and stopped. Some of the Japanese sailors were frightened at the strange sight and said that if it contained people like the ones in the old storybooks, it might be better not to trust themselves on board. But one of the crewmen had been to Nagasaki, where he had seen the black ships of the Dutch, and he said that the strange vessel must be a Hollander, either coming from or going to the trading port.

It took half an hour to lower the ship's boat and finish the necessary preparations to leave the old vessel forever. The Captain was hurried into the boat first, being the eldest; Heco was put on board next, being the youngest. The Japanese sculled their little boat toward the strange black vessel, which stood still, as if in port, waiting for them. The maneuver, heaving to by positioning the sails, was an astonishing feat of seamanship to the Japanese sailors.

The ship, the *Auckland,* was bound for San Francisco and the "gold mountain" which had recently been found in California. Everything about the black vessel was new, strange and frightening to the Japanese. The crew of eleven, consisting of a captain, two mates, six men, a cook and a boy, was outnumbered by the rescued Japanese, who totaled sixteen officers and men. The strangers on the mysterious vessel were mostly bearded, dressed in dark- or red-flannel shirts and black trousers, which the Oriental sailors had never seen before.

Storm on the coast, by Sesson (Nomura Collection, Kyoto)

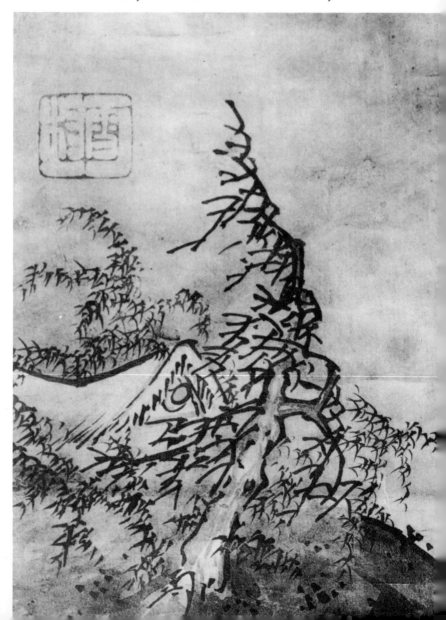

The captain of the *Auckland* showed charts to his rescued visitors and pointed to something called "Ah-me-ri-ka," which sounded familiar to some of the Japanese sailors who had seen Commodore Biddle's fleet in Edo Bay. Pointing to the chart and to the ship, the mate made it understood that the *Auckland* was American. He picked out a small section of the

chart which he called "Japan," adding "Edo" so that the shipwrecked sailors understood that he was making the connection with them. But to them the area shown seemed much too small to be Nippon—they had been taught that Japan was larger than most other countries.

The differences between the American and Japanese navigational instruments and methods struck the Orientals with amazement. The American compass had thirty-two points; the Japanese, only twelve. It took two, three and sometimes five men to handle the clumsy tiller on the Japanese ship; only one man was required at the wheel of the American bark. The instruments on the *Auckland* puzzled the Japanese. The captain and the mate took readings of the sun, a procedure which the Japanese did not understand. Some thought land was being sighted over the horizon, some thought that the distance to the sun was being measured, some considered the procedure a measurement of time. None guessed that the reading of the sun's altitude was to determine the ship's latitude.

Young Heco had difficulties adjusting to the odd customs of the bearded strangers. He was given bread with salt butter, the smell of which he found unbearable. Without realizing it, he ate beef, a great sin, the usual punishment for which was being forbidden to pray or worship for seventy-five days. He excused himself, however, on the grounds of ignorance, washed his hands, rinsed his mouth and turned westward to pray to the gods of Nippon to forgive his unwitting sin. One day at sea, the second mate came up to the young man, pointing to his own hair and to the topknot on young Heco's head. The lad thought he was comparing the color or style and nodded to be agreeable. The mate immediately got a pair of scissors and cut off the Japanese boy's topknot. This greatly distressed the lad because, while he was still on the Japanese wreck, he had pledged his topknot as an offering to his gods if he were saved. Once again he washed his hands and mouth and begged forgiveness for another unwitting sin.

After the midday meal, the captain and mate usually came on deck and paced back and forth. This was a custom of walking which the Japanese had never seen before and there was much discussion about it, some thinking that the Americans were measuring the speed of the vessel, others disagreeing, saying, "How could one ever measure the distance merely walking on the deck?" For some time there was no way to clear up the confusion.

In the morning the captain looked to the east with the same instrument he had used previously. The Japanese thought he was looking ahead for land as they had heard that in Holland there were powerful glasses that could see things thousands of miles off. Later the Japanese sailors learned that the captain was making observations to determine the ship's longitude. The mate was seen jotting something down in the logbook in English script, which to the Japanese looked like waves, running sideways, not up and down the page as in their own writing. Some thought the mate was copying down the number of waves he had looked at, others said he was just noting the distance the vessel had traveled which he had measured by his strange walking back and forth on the deck.

The shipwrecked Japanese were afraid that they had been rescued only to be eaten by these barbarians. But one day the ship's hold was seen laden with tea, sugar, spice and biscuits and their fear of being devoured disappeared.

After being out of sight of land for nearly a hundred days, the Japanese found themselves at last outside the harbor of San Francisco.

"For the first time I saw what a foreign city was like,"

wrote Heco. "The streets were broad and paved with stones and tiles, with side-walks for foot-passengers and the center of the way for horses and wheeled traffic. The houses were much larger than in our own country, some of them two or three stories high, built of brick and stone, and though some of them were of wood, still even they were large and spacious. There were numerous shops of all kinds, with goods displayed in large glass windows, hotels, restaurants, drinking places, horses, carts and carriages. And all the people looked busy and the place seemed much like the City of Edo with the exception of the carts which were here drawn by horses instead of by men or cows and bullocks as they are in our country."

In the streets of San Francisco he saw other sights that were strange and shocking. There was a "chain gang" of convicts digging in a hill close by. The large Negro driver of a delivery wagon frightened the young Japanese, who had never seen a black man before.

One day the shipwrecked Japanese crew was invited to a fancy-dress ball in San Francisco. Before entering the main ballroom, they were conducted into an antechamber, with velvet cushioned chairs, handsome window curtains and a large mirror on the wall. The Japanese sat down and to their surprise saw seated directly in front of them others of their countrymen, or so they thought for a moment, since they had never seen a mirror larger than twelve or fifteen inches in diameter.

In the meantime word had come back to San Francisco from Washington to take care of the Japanese sailors, since the opportunity could be used to negotiate a treaty of friendship with Japan by taking back the natives in an American man-of-war. The Japanese were kept in San Francisco for about a year, at the expense of the United States Government, while Commodore Perry's expedition was being equipped.

In February 1852 the U.S. Navy ship *St. Mary* picked up the Japanese sailors in San Francisco and set out for Hong Kong, where it expected to meet Commodore Perry's squadron. The *St. Mary* arrived on May 20, and after a two-day stay made for Macao, where it found the large paddle-steam frigate, the *Susquehanna*, the flagship of the United States Far Eastern squadron, then under the command of Commodore Aulick. The Japanese sailors were transferred to the *Susquehanna*, where they found the crew much different from the comfortable, friendly company of the *St. Mary*. The large American man-of-war had been in the China service for a long time and its officers and men had become accustomed to dealing with the Chinese in a contemptuous manner. The crew of the *Susquehanna* treated Heco and his companions brutally and scornfully as they did the Chinese.

"But in this they were wrong," wrote Heco. "For in our childhood we had been taught that man must respect man as man and not treat him like a beast. This treatment caused some of our elders to become very vexed. We kept silent, but anger began to smoulder in our breasts."

Some of the Japanese resolved to leave the American warship and find their way home by other means. One group of eight decided to go overland, while the rest determined to wait the coming of Perry and his ships. It was agreed that whichever party reached Japan first would report the safety of the others to families and friends. The overland party was immediately waylaid by highwaymen and the eight Japanese barely escaped with their lives. They returned to the *Susquehanna* in rags. There was nothing to do but to bear the humiliating atmosphere with patience.

But the days and weeks went by and still Commodore Perry did not put in an appearance. Tired of waiting, Heco resolved to go back to California, where the gold rush was still attracting men by the thousands. Perhaps he would later find a way to get back to Japan. Heco was given his leave and sailed on an old British bark, *Sarah Hooper,* arriving in San Francisco after a voyage of fifty days. This was in December 1852. Commodore Perry had sailed for Japan on the *Mississippi* on November 24.

The year 1852 was exactly three centuries and ten years since the first Westerner, the Portuguese adventurer Fernám Mendes Pinto, had touched Japan. In that time many travelers had come back and reported their observations of the country and the people. Nevertheless, movement inside Japan was so restricted that its reputation continued as a *terra incognita,* an unknown land.

One phenomenon, in particular, puzzled most Westerners. There seemed to be two emperors in Japan, one supposedly "spiritual," the other "secular," reigning contemporaneously over the land. Commodore Perry was to run directly into this situation when he steamed around the Cape of Good Hope, through the Indian Ocean to Hong Kong, Okinawa (the Ryukyus—then called Lew Chews), finally reaching Tokyo Bay. This dual political structure in Japan had developed over a period of nearly a thousand years, since 858 A.D., when Seiwa, a nine-year-old boy, became the fifty-sixth emperor of Japan. One of his ministers, a leader of the Fujiwara family, assumed full sovereign power, to be wielded in the name of the young emperor. For three centuries members of the Fujiwara family acted as hereditary regent whenever an emperor was a minor and as grand minister when he came of age.

The Fujiwara influence over the Japanese throne was replaced by the Taira; they held power from 1160 to 1185, when they were overthrown by the Minamoto. Yoritomo, first of the Minamoto Shoguns, established the center of his military administration at Kamakura and sent faithful retainers all over Japan to act as military magistrates and stewards. This military network, owing its allegiance to the Minamoto Shogun, became the basis of the Japanese feudal system, which was to last for the next seven centuries.

Yoritomo was appointed *Sei-i Tai-Shōgun,* or "commander in chief against the barbarians." The office had first been created by the fiftieth emperor, Kammu (781–806), to put down the revolt of the outlying tribes in the northern islands of Japan. Again, in the time of the fifty-second emperor, Saga (809-823), a *Sei-i Tai-Shōgun* was named to put down another insurrection. These were the only two occasions on which the office had been held before the time of Yoritomo. Originally it was not a hereditary post, but one that had been filled as the necessity arose. Since the border tribes were completely subdued by the end of the twelfth century, the title had lost its meaning of "barbarian-repelling generalissimo." It became instead the official designation of the chief of the feudal military government, and was made hereditary in the Minamoto family. The word *Sei-i Tai-Shōgun,* was abbreviated to *Shōgun.* This marked the real beginning of the Shogunate.

The Minamoto Shoguns were replaced early in the thirteenth century by the Hōjō, who ruled until 1333. In 1338 the Ashikaga seized the office and held it for more than two hundred years. The Tokugawa Shoguns assumed power in 1603 and ruled until 1867. The Tokugawa Shogun described by Thunberg in 1776 was Ieharu; when Commodore Perry arrived in 1853 the Shogun was Ieyoshi.

The Tokugawa Shoguns strengthened the feudal organizations of the Shogunate by gathering together all the lords, or *daimyō,* and making them swear allegiance to them in their castle at Edo. It was the Tokugawa Shoguns who first invited in the Spanish and English traders. It was also the Tokugawa Shoguns who established Japan's policy of national isolation and exterminated Christianity in the country.

Some of the Shoguns were farsighted and statesmanlike. They introduced elements of Western science and civilization into Japan. The importation of Dutch books on mathematics, astronomy, geography, medicine, botany and chemistry was encouraged. The study of Dutch was fostered, and scholars, particularly in the reign of the eighth Shogun, Yoshimune (1716–1745), were encouraged to publish translations of important Dutch works.

Yet, while the first half of the nineteenth century in the West brought new scientific developments, new inventions, and new industrial techniques, Japan remained behind locked

ports, secluded and aloof from the changing world. Western influences came closer and closer as England and France established themselves in Asia. The Russians also were making their presence felt. Even the Dutch, still clinging to their ancient trade monopoly at Deshima in the harbor of Nagasaki, suggested to Japan that it open itself to international commerce. The Dutch also forecast the approach of the Americans. The Japanese response was to bolster its weak coastal defenses with antiquated cannon cast from temple bells. Military discipline was copied from the Dutch and a national flag designed.

This generally was the state of affairs as the United States fleet, steaming in a line, arrived in Tokyo Bay in 1853, and dropped anchor off the port of Uraga.

The Minamoto Shogun, Yoritomo, hunting at the foot of Mount Fuji; detail of a wood-block print by Kiyomitsu (Courtesy, Museum of Fine Arts, Boston)

Left: *American warship in Japanese harbor; woodcut (Library of Congress)*

Right: *Matthew C. Perry, Japanese sketch (Collection Norfolk Museum of Arts and Sciences, Norfolk, Va.)*

2. COMMODORE PERRY:

DELIVERY OF THE PRESIDENT'S LETTER

The American naval expedition to Japan, which was to be led by Commodore Matthew C. Perry, was originally scheduled to sail in the spring of 1852. The war with Mexico had ended four years before with the transfer of the territory of California to the United States, so that the new nation now spanned the continent from the Atlantic to the Pacific. It naturally looked next to the Far East.

Direct trade between the West Coast of the United States and the markets in Asia was growing daily more practicable with the development of steam, but the new power required coal at convenient depots. Where was coal to be found on the long passage from California to China? Japan? The long-isolated island empire offered a tempting goal for American businessmen and traders, just as China had for the English. If Japan could be opened for commerce, many new opportunities would develop for America's rapidly expanding industries and merchant marine.

Many influential circles in the United States felt that Japan could not be permitted to remain behind her self-imposed barriers. It should be opened to international trade, by force if necessary. This view was presented by a New York newspaper, the *Express,* which spoke for sections of the commercial and financial community:

"Japan has no right to bury her treasures behind her walls, and to imprison her people under the cover of loathing and ignorant superstition. She must be made to feel that she is a power on the earth; that she has means, capacities and duties; and that if she fails in all of these, and *refuses to be enlightened, it is the duty of those who know her, even better than she knows herself, to force upon her the dawning of a better day.* So children are trained to their destiny and duty, and sometimes, through adversity, to the strength and glory of manhood." This attitude was also acknowledged in the official *Narrative of the Expedition of an American Squadron to the China Seas and Japan,* prepared under the supervision of Commodore Perry: "By some indeed the proposition was boldly avowed that Japan had no right thus to cut herself off from the community of nations; and that what she would not yield to national comity should be wrested from her by force."

But not all of America shared this belligerent opinion. The preparations for the expedition were secret, but inklings began to appear in the press early in the year. *The New York Times,* which had been founded the year before, urged a more moderate approach. In early February 1852 the newspaper editorialized: "The act, in the shape which rumor gives it, would be a virtual declaration of war." The pretext given for the display of force—that American sailors were being imprisoned and mistreated in Japan—was not satisfactorily proven, the *Times* declared, adding that if it turned out to be true, the sailors would probably be found guilty of violating the laws of Japan, in which case America had no right to interfere. It had never been the practice of the American government to attempt to protect its citizens by armed expeditions, the newspaper pointed out, adding:

"But, it is urged by the *Express,* Japan 'has no right' to shut herself up from intercourse with mankind; and therefore her ports should be opened violently, like so many oysters.

"This won't do at all. The President and the people of the United States are unanimous upon one point at least, and it is that 'one nation has no right to intervene in the domestic concerns of another.'"

The *Times* went on to disagree with the view that England's war with China (1841–42), which had succeeded in opening China's ports, set any kind of example for the way

America should act toward Japan. The newspaper's opinion was expressed somewhat sarcastically:

"The war ended, the result obtained, China has received the full benefit of the kindness: for every missionary admitted agreeably to the treaty, there has been a million dollars worth of opium introduced in spite of the treaty. And for every soul reclaimed by the devoted missionary effort, tens of thousands have been lost through the effects of that frightful poison."

By the end of the same month (February), however, *The New York Times* began to see the outlines of the Perry expedition more clearly. The New York newspaper continued its opposition, stating that it thought a "good diplomatic agent" was preferable to a show of armed force. Its editorial opinion of February 24, 1852, showed a slight change in tone.

"If we are to judge from the 'pomp and circumstance' with which rumor is clothing the preparations for this expedition, it is easy to perceive what the nature of these instructions are. A fleet composed of several steamers, backed by a frigate and one or two corvettes, is by no means a peaceful demonstration; and we fear that the effect of the arrival of these ships in the waters of Japan will be to frighten the poor Japanese out of their seaport towns, and out of their wits at the same time, so that it will be impossible to bring them to terms in good faith. They may be driven by their alarm into a treaty of some sort, which they will feel at perfect liberty to violate so soon as the vessels of war shall have been removed."

To fortify American support for the armed expedition to Japan reports were circulated of the imprisonment and mistreatment of American sailors in Japan. Even so, according to the *Times,* war was not called for. If American seamen were being abused, an opinion which it was inclined to doubt three weeks before, the situation could be resolved peaceably. "In treating with a barbarous people, some attempt should be made, we think, to obtain their confidence and good will, before resorting to force. An indemnity of some kind would probably be made as soon as demanded and satisfaction to the utmost extent yielded were negotiations properly conducted."

The expedition did not sail on schedule. Delay followed delay, while public opinion continued divided. In June the attitude of the *Times* seemed to be changing. It printed a story of the ill treatment of American sailors, which was curious because the news item was six years old. The newspaper story was in the form of a statement by one of the shipwrecked sailors from the *Lawrence* (1846), who was quoted as saying: "We were thrust into a prison cage, similar to those in which wild beasts are kept for exhibition." The sailor ended with a call for vengeance: "It is anxiously hoped that the American Government will not suffer this treatment towards hapless shipwrecked American seamen to pass without ample retribution."

The American expedition to Japan was originally slated for the command of Commodore J. A. Aulick, who never got the enterprise under way. In his stead, command was turned over to Commodore Matthew Calbraith Perry, brother of Oliver Hazard Perry, the naval hero of the 1813 Battle of Lake Erie against the British—"We have met the enemy and they are ours." Matthew C. Perry, himself a noted veteran of several campaigns, including the war with Mexico, was said to have preferred command of the American naval squadron in the Mediterranean, but once chosen for the Japanese mission, he devoted himself to his task. First he set himself to learning all that he could about Japan; above all he wanted to understand as much as possible the reasons for the country's unusual state of self-imposed isolation. First he turned to the history books and examined the record of the efforts of the Portuguese, the Russians and the English to break down the barriers. He searched out what seemed to him the secret of their failures: attempts to bully a brave people into submission and lack of understanding of the true character of the Japanese. Perry described the Japanese temperament as quick to distinguish between obsequiousness and true moderation, ready always to do what is kind and just, but never submitting for a second to anything considered insulting.

Perry offered another reason which he believed put the United States in a more favorable position to deal with the Japanese than the countries of Europe. Japan and the older countries of the West had had histories of unpleasant experiences for centuries; only the newer United States could claim that it had never displayed a hostile gesture toward Japan. The suspicion of treachery hung over the Portuguese in Japan for years. Just the hint that an English king had married a Portuguese princess was enough to break off any dealing between the two countries. In more recent times the English had outraged the Japanese by permitting the armed *Phaeton* to chase a Dutch prize into the neutral waters of Nagasaki Bay. The raids by the Russians on the islands of Sakhalin and the Kuriles in 1806 and 1807 had inspired Japanese ill will. Perry was of the opinion that the Dutch, who still carried on their trade monopoly, had submitted to insult, imprisonment and degradation for so long that the Japanese had little respect for any Westerner.

As far as Commodore Biddle's expedition (1846) was concerned, it was dismissed by Perry as "the only effort we made

Japan's mythical first emperor, whose reign was dated in the seventh century B.C.; *detail of triptych by Shosai Ginko (Museum of Fine Arts, Boston: Gift of Mr. and Mrs. Harold A. Curtis)*

Heroic twelfth century Taira general who leaped into the
sea rather than surrender; detail of the "Ghost of Tomomori,"
by Utagawa Kuniyoshi (Museum of Fine Arts, Boston: Bigelow
Collection)

towards friendly relations and it scarcely deserves the name."

The Perry expedition, of course, had the full backing of the highest United States officials, including President Millard Fillmore, Secretary of State Daniel Webster and his successor, John P. Kennedy. The Commodore was vested with extraordinary powers, diplomatic as well as naval. His mission was carefully spelled out: to procure friendly admission to Japan for the purpose of trade and to establish, at appropriate places, permanent coaling stations to supply American steamers crossing the Pacific. He was to carry an official letter from the President of the United States to the Emperor of Japan in which these objectives were set forth.

When it became known that Perry was definitely going to Japan, he was deluged with requests from all over the world from writers, scientists and adventure-seekers, eager to accompany him. Perry refused them all. He later explained his refusal on several grounds, the most important being that he felt his mission to be naval and diplomatic, not scientific; he was afraid that if he tried to do everything he would succeed in nothing. He admitted also that he did not want to be faced with the problem which would have come up from the presence on his ship of civilian scientists and literary men, not under the strict discipline of the navy. The Commodore's official instructions were to prohibit his staff and crew from giving out news of the squadron's movements to the press. Orders were even given that private letters to friends and families were to make no mention of this topic. All journals, diaries and notebooks kept by anyone connected with the expedition were considered the property of the government. They could not be published until officially released by the Navy Department. All these restrictions were necessary, the *Narrative* claimed, in order to keep any information away from rival European powers that might endanger the success of the American effort. Perry knew too that men of science were always writing letters to other scientists, asking questions, passing along new information, and he did not want to be in the position of having to censor such correspondence.

The Commodore had an additional motive: to encourage his own officers and men to make scientific observations. Perry's staff included officers with reputations as scientists and he wanted them to continue their efforts. When all the material was finally put into published form, it was done under his personal direction, with the Reverend Francis L. Hawks, rector of Calvary Church, New York, a widely traveled author, historian and biographer, acting as editor.

Finally, tired of the long delays, Perry decided not to wait in the United States for his entire squadron. On November 24, 1852, he sailed out of Norfolk, his broad pennon flying from the mast of his flagship, *Mississippi,* bound for Japan.

As he steamed across the Atlantic toward the Azores, there was no way of knowing what might happen if the Japanese resisted and he found himself forced to use his fleet's cannon. Other countries kept a watchful eye on his progress.

In January 1853 a French publication, *Annales du Commerce Extérieur,* was reported to express strong support of the American move: "It is easy to predict the answer which will be obtained by a demonstration that rests on eight armed ships of war—that is to say, one line-of-battle ship, three steam frigates and four corvettes; a complete, equipped squadron carrying not less than 219 guns.

"In like manner as China had to open up her trade before the English cannon, so must Japan cave in before the irresistible arguments the Americans will employ. America's conduct, it is true, has about it an energy which, at first glance, appears slightly brutal, but less so on the whole, than is the

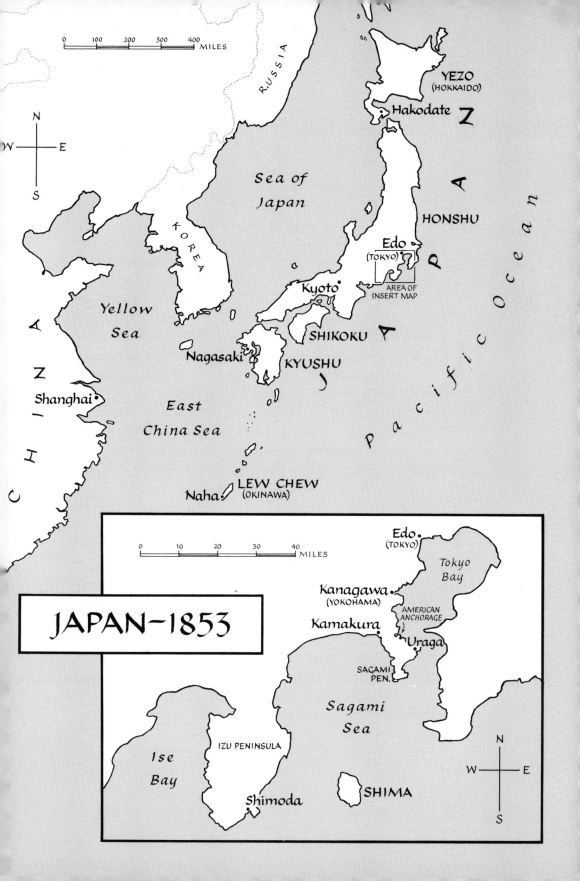

barbarous usage of these Orientals who persist in interdicting wandering vessels from their shores. Viewed in this light, we cannot but applaud this commercial crusade undertaken by the United States."

On the other side of the world, in Shanghai, a twenty-eight-year old American traveler and writer, Bayard Taylor, waited for Perry's arrival. Early in May 1853 Perry finally reached Shanghai, where, with much firing of salutes, he transferred his Commodore's pennant to the big paddle-wheeled *Susquehanna*. The greater part of Shanghai, according to Taylor, flocked to the harbor to witness the ceremonies. Perry's presence and that of his officers "gave a fresh impetus to the social activity of the foreign population. Thenceforth there were balls, dinners, and other entertainments in great abundance."

Active preparations for the squadron's departure for Japan were begun immediately, and by the middle of the month the steamers were scheduled to depart. Taylor wanted to accompany the expedition to Japan, but he soon learned of the edict against civilian passengers. According to Taylor's own account, there existed in the Navy at that time the rating of master's-mate, and there were two vacancies which the Commodore had the power to fill. Taylor agreed to enter the naval service temporarily with that rank and, having signed his articles of allegiance, became an officer of "moderate rank, with unlimited respect for my superiors, and the reverse for my inferiors." He understood that he would have to surrender every journal, note, sketch or observation of any kind made during the cruise. Many passages from his journal were included in the final *Narrative*. Other acting master's-mates on the *Mississippi*, according to Taylor, were William Heine, the artist, William B. Draper, in charge of the telegraph apparatus, and Eliphalet Brown, Jr., the daguerreotypist. Another of the same rating was Dr. James Morrow, a physician who was interested in tropical botany. Accompanying the expedition also were the interpreters S. Wells Williams for Chinese and Antón Portman for Dutch.

Commodore Perry's visit to Naha, the principal port of Okinawa, was in the nature of a rehearsal. The American commodore-diplomat was determined to test some carefully planned tactics with the rulers of the Ryukyu Islands: refusal to treat with anyone but personages of rank at least equal to his own; formal but friendly attitudes; payment for all goods and services; no delaying or temporizing. At Naha, Commodore Perry succeeded in arranging a meeting with the island official who was called the regent. The American then insisted upon paying a courtesy call in return at the Royal Palace, though every effort was made to divert him. Perry's general plan seemed to be working.

On the morning of July 2, 1853, the American fleet quit the harbor of Naha. The squadron was now reduced to only four vessels: the two steamers, the flagship *Susquehanna* and the *Mississippi,* and the sloops-of-war *Saratoga* and *Plymouth.*

"This was but a poor show of ships, in comparison with the more imposing squadron of twelve vessels which had been repeatedly promised," complained the *Narrative.* "But as none of these additional vessels had arrived, and as no calculation could be made as to when they might be looked for, the Commodore resolved to sail with the inferior force."

The advantage of steam was very apparent, for the *Susquehanna* took the *Saratoga* in tow, and the steamer *Mississippi* towed the *Plymouth.* The small fleet was at sea on the Fourth of July 1853, the seventy-seventh anniversary of the founding of the United States. The occasion was to be celebrated by some amateur theatricals on shipboard, but the weather turned unfavorable and it was deemed wise to cancel the show. In-

北亞墨利加人物

ペルリ像

Commodore Perry—a Japanese point of view; print (Library of Congress)

stead, a salute of seventeen guns from each vessel was fired and the crew got an extra ration of grog. There was a holiday feeling, if only in the respite from the usual drills and exercises on which the Commodore insisted. He was determined that everyone be prepared for any eventuality in Japan.

At sunset on July 7 the squadron approached Cape Izu, and by morning land could be seen from the masthead. The Americans' first view of the coast was blurred by a haze, but through the mist, the bold headland rose loftily, stretching back into the interior. The *Susquehanna*, leading the squad-

Commodore Perry —an official American portrait by John Beaufain Irving (United States Naval Academy Museum)

ron, set its course directly for the entrance of the bay of Edo. As the vessels sailed up along the coast, eight or ten Japanese boats came into sight; immediately two or three changed course and headed back to shore, as if to announce the arrival of the strangers.

Through the morning haze, past shrouded shorelines, the big ships moved steadily up the bay. They were probably the first steamships the Japanese had ever seen, and the crews of the fishing boats stood up and gaped with astonishment as the fleet continued against the wind, all sails furled, moving at the rate of eight or nine knots an hour. As the day advanced, the sun dispelled the mist, disclosing majestic Mount Fuji, its conelike summit soaring into the sky.

As the ships neared the bay of Sagami, Perry ordered the decks cleared for action. Guns were positioned and loaded. Small arms were distributed, sentinels were posted and preparations made as if to meet a possible enemy. When the American squadron was within two miles of land, a great number of Japanese boats pushed off in its direction. The squadron did not wait and the boats were soon left behind, their crews puzzled by the steamers' speed. The Japanese boats were fully manned but did not seem to be armed; each carried a large banner, inscribed with certain characters, which led the Americans to believe that they were government vessels of some kind.

Beyond Cape Sagami, the shoreline rose in precipitous cliffs, which connected landward with a pleasant, rolling countryside. At first glance the entrance to Sagami Bay seemed well fortified. The hills and projecting headlands all around looked formidable, with forts and guns, which nonetheless remained silent. The squadron passed through the straits into the inner bay of Uraga, making numerous fishing boats scurry out of the way, and reached its anchorage in the late afternoon. The wind having turned favorable, the sloops had been cast loose and all four vessels took up positions opposite the shore.

Since Perry did not consider the navigating charts of Edo Bay very trustworthy, there was constant sounding ahead of the ships to determine the depth of the water. The bay was found to have a safe draft of twenty-five fathoms, which continued almost to the promontory guarding the entrance to the inner harbor of Edo. Perry's ships had gone a mile farther into the harbor than any previous foreign vessel, or so he estimated, when two guns from a nearby fort were fired and rockets discharged. The steamers, after closing in a little with the shore, dropped their anchors. Perry had positioned his ships so that their guns commanded the entire shore as well as two towns of some size.

The moment of the first testing was at hand. Perry had given the strictest orders that no one was to be admitted aboard any but his own flagship, and then not more than three persons at one time with business on board. Since in the past all visitors had generally been allowed, the first Japanese who came out to the American anchorage showed annoyance when they were not permitted to come aboard. But the Commodore's orders were strict.

After the American squadron had dropped anchor, another gun was heard from one of the forts somewhere on shore, and a large number of guard boats came from all directions, evidently ordered by the signal to surround the foreign ships. The crews, with ample provisions of water, clothing, sleeping mats and other materials, seemed prepared for a long stay. Perry, however, had made up his mind beforehand that he would not let his ships be besieged. The Japanese made several attempts to get alongside the *Saratoga,* but whatever lines they tied onto the ship were unceremoniously cast off. Japanese crewmen tried to climb the anchor chains, but the American seamen met them with pikes, cutlasses and pistols, and drove them back. The Japanese soon gave up trying to board the ships.

One of the Japanese boats came alongside the flagship. On board was a person with a scroll of paper in his hand, which the officers of the *Susquehanna* refused to accept. Held up and read aloud alongside the *Mississippi,* it proved to be an

View of Mount Fuji, by Katsushika Hokusai
(Courtesy, Museum of Fine Arts, Boston)

order in French for the ships to anchor only at their peril. The chief personage on the boat made signs to be permitted on board the *Susquehanna,* but he was refused.

The conversation was carried on in Dutch, which the Japanese official spoke fluently. He asked if the ships came from America, as though he had expected them. He kept trying to get permission to come on board, but was as constantly rejected with the statement that Perry was of the highest rank and could confer only with the highest ranking Japanese in Uraga. The Japanese spokesman pointed to an official the Americans thought was the Vice-Governor of Uraga. Why did the Governor not come? the Americans asked. He replied that it was contrary to law for a chief magistrate to board ships in the harbor. It was then proposed that an officer of equal rank with the vice-magistrate be appointed to confer with him. Perry agreed and named his aide, Lieutenant John Contee. The Japanese official was received in the captain's cabin, and a conference held. The talk was, in fact, with Commodore Perry, who did not show himself, but remained secluded in his own cabin, communicating with the Japanese through his flag lieutenant.

At this conference, the Japanese official was informed that Commodore Perry had been sent by the American government on a friendly mission to Japan, that he had brought a letter from the President of the United States, addressed to the Emperor of Japan, and that he wished an officer of suitable rank to be appointed for the Commodore formally to deliver the original of the letter. The Japanese officer replied that, according to the laws of Japan, Nagasaki was the only place for negotiating business with foreigners and the squadron should therefore go there. He was answered that the Commodore had intentionally come to Uraga because it was close to Edo and that the American fleet would under no circumstances move to Nagasaki. Perry let it be known through his aide that he expected the President's letter to be received properly where he was, that his intentions were friendly, and that he would permit no insult either to him or to his squadron. Guard boats would not be suffered to collect around the ships, and the official was then notified that unless they were immediately dispersed, he would drive them off by force. The Japanese official immediately went to the ship's gangway and issued an order, which sent most of the boats back to shore. A few still remained, so an American boat was lowered with an armed contingent to warn them away. The remaining Japanese boats took the hint, disappeared, and nothing more was seen of them during the squadron's stay. This, Commodore Perry felt, was the first important point that he had gained.

Perry's strategy, as it was outlined in the *Narrative of the Expedition,* was to assume a firm attitude toward the Japanese government and its officials. He had made up his mind to take the opposite course of all the others who had preceded him to Japan on similar errands, that is, to demand "as a right, not as a favor," the acts of courtesy normal between civilized nations. Whether, as a last resort, he would have to force his way ashore, was a question he left to events. It was the last action he desired, but, to be ready for the worst, all ships were kept on constant alert, the crews continuously drilled as though at war.

The Commodore's judgment proved sound, for the American squadron was not subjected to the annoying forms of surveillance that all foreign ships had endured for more than two hundred years. There were still watchful eyes, but they were at a distance. The American ships were probably under observation from the shore also. During the afternoon three

American landing at Uraga, 1853; Japanese print
(The Mariners Museum, Newport News, Va.)

or four rockets were fired, which were probably signals of some sort. That night beacon fires were lit on both the highlands and along the shores, and all through the dark hours the tolling of a great bell could be heard, which was taken to be an alarm of some kind. When the Commodore's flagship, however, fired its nine o'clock gun, a sixty-four pounder, the report echoed and reechoed through the hills along the western side of the bay. Some of the signal fires were immediately extinguished, but otherwise the Americans found no reason to be alarmed. Every ship was fully prepared, on the alert and ready for action; sentinels were stationed fore and aft and on the gangways; every gun was ready with a pile of round shot and four stands of grapeshot; muskets were stacked on the quarter deck; and the small boats were armed with carbines, pistols and cutlasses.

The next morning, as the sun gradually burned away the mist over the bay, fortifications could be seen on the hills and headlands that commanded the harbor. They were examined through the telescope and found to be in sad condition, some unfinished, others in states of construction or alteration. Some seemed to have cannon, some were without a gun. Companies of soldiers, wearing bright red uniforms, were observed moving from garrison to garrison, carrying flags and large lanterns on tall poles. The flotilla of government boats was lined up near the shore.

Early the next morning a boatload of artists came close to the flagship, but no attempt was made to come on board. Instead the artists busied themselves making sketches of the strange "black ships." Soon two large boats were rowed alongside, each carrying half a dozen official-looking persons, including, it was announced, the official of the highest authority in the city. This person, named Eizaemon Kayama, presented himself as the Magistrate, or leading functionary of Uraga, directly contradicting the statement of his subordinate the day previous that officials of his rank were not permitted aboard ships in the harbor. His presence was announced to Perry, who ordered Commanders Buchanan and Adams, as well as Lieutenant Contee, to receive him. The Commodore still refused to see anyone lower in rank than a councilor of the Empire.

The discussion between the Japanese official and the American officers went over the same ground: that Japanese law forbade intercourse with strangers anywhere but in Nagasaki, that even if the letter were delivered in Uraga, the answer would be returned in Nagasaki, so the squadron might as well go there at once. The Commodore, in his cabin, kept in close touch with the discussions; he let it be known that he would never consent to these limitations. The letter from the American President would be delivered where the squadron was; if the Japanese government did not appoint a suitable person to receive the friendly letter, addressed to the Emperor of Japan, the Americans would go ashore and deliver it themselves, by force if necessary. After much discussion, it was agreed that a request for instructions would be sent to Edo and that a reply would be expected in three or four days.

Every morning, at daylight, each ship of the squadron had sent out small boats to survey the bay and harbor of Uraga. The Japanese official protested these examinations of Japanese waters as against the laws of the land, but Perry persisted, declaring that he was bound by American law, which commanded him to insure the safety of his ships. "This," remarked the Commodore, "was a second and most important point gained."

Early on Monday morning, July 11, the surveying boats were ordered to go higher up in the bay, closer to Edo itself, and the steamer *Mississippi* was directed to get underway to protect them. The Commodore's purpose was to make the approach of the powerful ship press the government in Edo for a quicker and more favorable answer to his request. The ship's movement up the bay brought Kayama rushing out to the flagship to find out the reason. He was told that if the business of the President's letter could not be accomplished during this present visit, the Commodore would have to come back the following year with even more ships, and that he needed a

better anchorage than the one before Uraga, which he considered neither convenient nor safe. He wanted to be closer to Edo to make communication with that city easier.

That day the situation grew tense as the surveying boats proceeded ten or twelve miles farther toward Edo. The *Mississippi* followed two miles behind; but the whole squadron

A critical moment: American surveying party opposed by fleet of Japanese boats; lithograph by William Heine, official artist to the expedition (Library of Congress)

was alerted for any emergency. Steam was raised in the *Sus-quehanna* in case of need. On shore a force of a thousand Japanese soldiers marched down to the beach and embarked in boats which headed for the surveying party. All the forts seemed active with the movement of troops. The Japanese boats tried to wave off the American surveyors, and the Americans stopped rowing and fixed their bayonets. But the Japanese were not frightened off until the *Mississippi* came up with its heavy armament. The bay was found to be navigable to the farthest point that the Americans reached, and they believed that big ships could safely get to within a few miles of Edo itself.

The day set to receive the Japanese government reply from Edo came at last. It was Tuesday, July 12. At about half past nine, three boats pulled out from Uraga and approached the flagship *Susquehanna*. On board one was Kayama, dressed in rich silken robes. He was immediately received with all formality and ushered into the presence of Captains Buchanan and Adams. Kayama informed the American naval officers that a building would be erected on shore to receive the Commodore and his staff and that a high personage, appointed by the Emperor, would receive the letter from the American President. He added, however, that no answer would be given in the bay of Edo; it would be sent to Nagasaki and forwarded by the Dutch or Chinese trading agents there.

In response, the Commodore wrote a memorandum which was immediately translated into Dutch and fully explained to Kayama. It said: "The Commander-in-Chief will not go to Nagasaki, and will receive no communication through the Dutch or Chinese. He has a letter from the President of the United States to deliver to the Emperor of Japan or to his secretary of foreign affairs, and he will deliver the original to none other. If this friendly letter of the President to the Emperor is not received and duly replied to, he will consider his country insulted, and will not hold himself accountable for the consequences. He expects a reply of some sort in a few days and he will receive such reply nowhere but in this neighborhood"— meaning the Bay of Uraga.

This memorandum sent the Japanese officials back to shore to consult higher authorities. They returned in the afternoon to report that a high officer would arrive in two days to receive the letter in a special reception house to be built on shore at Kurihama, just below Uraga.

"Will the high officer who will come here be accredited by the Emperor to receive the letters from the Admiral?" asked Captain Buchanan. Perry was referred to as an admiral since that rank was familiar to the Japanese.

"He has the authorization of the Emperor," replied Kayama. "He will receive the letter, but cannot enter into any negotiations."

A statement by Captain Buchanan was then written down in Dutch and handed to the Japanese interpreter. It read:

"The Admiral is now willing to meet with a high officer of Yedo, holding rank in Japan corresponding to the rank of Admiral in the United States. This officer shall be accredited, that is: possess a writing properly signed by the Emperor, authorizing him to receive the letters. Of this writing or letter of credence shall be made a copy, translated into Dutch, and the same copy to be transmitted to the Admiral before the interview takes place.

"At this interview there shall be no discussions whatever; no more than an exchange of civilities and compliments.

"The Admiral does not insist upon receiving an answer to the original letter of the President immediately, but will come back for that purpose after some months."

"When will he come for a reply?" Buchanan was asked.

"He will return in a few months," was the answer.

After the conference was over, the Japanese were guests of the officers of the *Susquehanna*. The Japanese officials were inclined to be friendly and social, though at all times they kept an air of dignity. They shared freely and gaily in the conversation, displaying themselves generally well informed. They were expert linguists, knowing Dutch and Chinese, and were quite familiar with the geography of the world and the science of the time. They were shown a globe and the United States was pointed out to them; they immediately put their fingers on Washington and New York, perfectly aware of the fact that one was the capital and the other the commercial center of the United States. The Japanese knew the locations of England, France, Denmark and the other kingdoms of Europe. They asked questions about the United States which showed they knew a good deal about the growth and development of the country. They asked if it was not true that Americans cut roads through mountains, referring, it was supposed, to the new railroad tunnels. They asked questions about a canal which was supposed to be cut across the Isthmus of Panama, referring, or so Perry's officers thought, to the railroad which was then being constructed. The Japanese knew something was being built to connect the two oceans and they referred to it as a canal, never having seen a railroad.

The Japanese officials showed great interest in the setup of the American warships, observing the big guns and, according to the *Narrative*, exhibiting "none of that surprise which would naturally be expected from those beholding for the first time the wonderful art and mechanism of a perfected steamship." They were particularly interested in the workings of the big engines, and they also showed that they had some knowledge of its principles.

The Japanese guests remained on board until evening, when they left the ship, bowing at every step, smiling in a friendly but dignified manner. The Americans realized that the ceremonial politeness was not put on for their benefit because the Japanese bowed to one another as soon as they entered their boats as though they were meeting for the first time.

The day for the meeting of Perry and the Japanese high official was set for July 14. In preparation, all captains were summoned on board the flagship. Orders were issued that the squadron was to move early in the morning and to anchor in a line that would command the whole bay in front of the reception place. Perry could not be sure that an elaborate trap was not being set for him and he was determined to be ready for any treachery. He was also resolved to present as colorful a show as possible and ordered all officers and men who could be spared from ship duty to appear in full uniform to make up his retinue.

The appointed day dawned with an obscured sky, but the sun soon came through warm and bright and dispelled the fog and cloud banks which shrouded the shores. During the night the Japanese, too, had been busy in preparation. Ornamental cloth screens had been set up to emphasize the power of the shore batteries and forts. The screens were emblazoned with coats of arms. Flags and pennants of varied designs and colors decorated the screens, behind which throngs of soldiers were seen, dressed in new uniforms.

On the American ships all was alert since the first dawning. Steam was got up and the anchors weighed. There was no wind, so the sailing vessels could not be moved into position. The officers, seamen and marines who were to accompany the Commodore were mustered, adding up to a complement of almost three hundred men. The American officers were in full official dress; the sailors and marines wore blue and white uniforms.

Early in the morning the two steamers, the *Susquehanna* and the *Mississippi,* moved slowly down the bay. At the very same time, six Japanese boats sailed on a parallel course closer to shore. Two flew the striped flag of the government boats, indicating the presence on board of important dignitaries, while the others carried red banners which were thought to show that they were carrying guards and soldiers.

When the ships rounded the headland, the Americans could see the preparations on shore. Along the head of the bay was a long stretch of gaily painted screens, emblazoned with the Shogun's arms, which Perry thought were those of the Emperor. Nine tall standards were erected in the middle of an immense number of banners of the richest colors. The whole effect was a crescent of variously colored flags, which fluttered brightly in the rays of the morning sun. In front of this display, ranged along the beach, were regiments of Japanese soldiers, standing in fixed order, evidently "to give an appearance of martial force, that the Americans might be duly impressed with the military power of the Japanese." Away from the beach, back from the center of the curved shore of the bay, stood the building which had been constructed for Perry's reception. It rose high above surrounding houses, with its three pyramid-shaped roofs which reminded the Commodore of "a group of very large ricks of grain." The building was covered in front by striped cloth, which extended in screens to either side.

As the American steamers neared the mouth of the bay, two Japanese boats approached the *Susquehanna.* Kayama and his interpreters came aboard, followed immediately by the official who had been called the Vice-Magistrate of Uraga. All were dressed in full official costume, with elaborately decorated gowns of rich silk brocade, gaily colored, with yellow velvet and embroidered with gold lace.

At a signal from the flagship, the boats from the other ships pulled up with the officers, sailors and marines. The fifteen launches and cutters were an imposing sight, as Captain Buchanan led the way, flanked by the two Japanese escort boats. As the boats moved, the bands of both steamers began to play. When the boats were halfway to the shore, thirteen guns on the *Susquehanna* began to boom away, reechoing among the hills, announcing that Commodore Perry was stepping into his barge to be rowed to the shore.

Captain Buchanan, commanding the advance party, was the first to spring ashore, the first American to land officially in the Japanese Empire. He was followed by a hundred marines from the other boats, who marched up a temporary wharf, built of bags of sand and straw, and formed a line on either side, facing the sea. Then came a hundred sailors, who also moved in formation, while the two ships' bands brought up the rear.

The Japanese force around the reception area was said to be five thousand, but seemed far greater. It was extended in a line around the whole beach, while a great number of men were hidden behind the cover of the cloth screens in the back. The Japanese soldiers did not appear to the Americans as well disciplined, but they were fairly well armed with swords, spears and matchlocks. In front were footsoldiers, archers and lancers; behind them were large bodies of cavalry, somewhat in the distance, as though being held in reserve. Besides the troops, a large number of Japanese people, among them many women, stood quietly watching the strange visitors from the other side of the world.

When Perry landed, his officers formed a double line along the wharf and fell into order behind him as he passed. The pro-

彼理上陸断

コンマンダント指揮之

The Commodore and his standard-bearer come ashore, and
Marines in drill formation; watercolor scroll (Collection Norfolk
Museum of Arts and Sciences, Norfolk, Va.)

cession moved toward the reception house, with the Marines
leading the way, the sailors following. The Stars and Stripes
and the Commodore's pennant were carried by two brawny
seamen. Two boys, dressed for the occasion, walked before the
Commodore, bearing in an envelope of scarlet cloth the boxes
in which the President's letters and the Commodore's creden-
tials were contained. These documents were written on vellum
and bound in blue silk velvet. The seals, attached by cords of
gold and silk with hanging gold tassels, were encased in round

銃卒胴塚

boxes, made of pure gold. Each document, together with its seal, was in a rosewood box, with lock, hinges and mountings all of gold.

On either side of the Commodore marched a tall Negro-American, fully armed, who was serving as his personal body-guard. Specially chosen for the occasion, they were two of the best-looking men in the squadron. "All this, of course," says the *Narrative of the Expedition,* "was but for effect."

The way to the entrance of the reception house was slightly roundabout, which permitted an even greater display for the Commodore and his escort. Before the entrance of the house were two small brass cannon, old and apparently of European make. On either side, too, were rather straggling companies of Japanese guards, uniformed differently from the other soldiers. They were armed with muskets, flintlocks and old-fashioned matchlocks.

Having been escorted to the door, the Commodore entered the building with his staff. The house itself showed that it had been put together hastily. The pine timbers and boarding were numbered, as though they had been precut and reassembled at the site. The first part of the structure was a kind of tent made of painted canvas. A carpet led from the entrance hall to an inner apartment, which was the official reception hall. Its floor was raised, like a dais, and elaborately decorated. The walls on three sides were hung with violet silks and fine cottons, embroidered with coats of arms in white.

As the Commodore came into the reception hall, two dignitaries sitting on the left rose and bowed. Perry and his suite were conducted to armchairs on the right. The names and titles of the Japanese dignitaries, as Perry recorded them, were Toda, Izu-no-kami and Ido, Iwami-no-kami. The title "no-kami," literally translated as "of lord," has no precise equivalent in English; in Perry's time it corresponded roughly to "the honorable," representing high position or important office. Commodore Perry's interpreters translated the title as "prince," and later writers as "lord of."

Both Toda and Ido were men of years, one around fifty, the other sixty or more. The younger, Toda, seemed amiable and intelligent. Both were richly dressed in heavy silk brocades, woven with elaborate figures in gold and silver. Both sat with an air of formality which they maintained throughout the ceremony. They never uttered a word, and rose from their seats only when the Commodore came in and again when he left. Both times they greeted him with a grave and formal bow. The two lords were the actual magistrates of Uraga.

Kayama and his interpreters, acting as masters of ceremonies, knelt beside a large red lacquered box. The silence was broken by the principal Japanese interpreter, who turned to the Americans' Dutch-speaking interpreter, Mr. Portman, and asked whether the letters from the President and the Commodore were ready for delivery. The scarlet box was pointed out as the receptacle for the letters. Perry beckoned to the boys, who were waiting in the entrance hall, to come forward. The two stalwart Negroes stepped smartly forward, took the letters from the boys, displayed the writing and seals and then rested the documents on the lid of the Japanese box. The whole ceremony took place in perfect silence.

After each of the letters had been explained, Kayama approached the silent Japanese dignitaries, and prostrating himself before them, received a scroll which was then ceremoniously delivered to Perry.

The Dutch interpreter asked the kneeling Japanese: "What papers are these?"

"They are the Imperial receipt," was the answer.

The translation of the receipt given to Commodore Perry read:

"The letter of the President of the United States of North America, and copy, are hereby received, and will be delivered to the Emperor.

"It has been many times intimated that business relating to foreign countries cannot be transacted here in Uraga, but at Nagasaki; nevertheless, as it has been observed that the Admiral, in his quality of ambassador of the President, would feel himself insulted by a refusal to receive the letter at this place, the justice of which has been acknowledged, the above mentioned letter is hereby received, in opposition to the Japanese law.

"As this is not a place wherein to negotiate with foreigners, so neither can conferences nor entertainment be held. Therefore, as the letter has been received, you can depart."

After another silence of several moments, the Commodore informed the Japanese officials that he would leave in two or three days, and advised them that his intention was to return to Japan in the following spring, probably in April or May.

The question was asked whether he would return with all four vessels.

"All of them," answered Perry, "and probably more, as these are only a portion of the squadron."

The whole ceremony had not taken more than twenty or thirty minutes. It had been conducted with the utmost formality and courtesy.

The American procession re-formed before the reception building and the Commodore was escorted to his barge; he boarded it and was rowed off toward his ship. The other Americans followed after some delay because of the small size of the temporary wharf, which had been hemmed in by sixty or seventy Japanese government boats. At the same time many Japanese soldiers crowded in from various parts of the beach, either to satisfy their curiosity or to present a fiercer front. Commodore Perry later admitted that the Japanese could easily have overwhelmed the American landing party if they had wanted to.

But before setting out that morning, Perry had positioned his two steamers so that they commanded the little bay. The decks had been cleared and everything was ready. Howitzers had been set up in boats alongside, which were prepared to go into action if trouble developed on shore. The ships' guns were primed and targeted on the line of Japanese troops in case hostilities started.

The reception over, every man in the squadron could relax and share the general satisfaction. In the customary relationship between two nations, not much had happened: two official letters had been delivered and their receipt acknowledged. But in the face of Japan's long policy of isolation, Perry felt there was every reason for self-satisfaction. The *Narrative of the Expedition* notes that in the phrase "opposition to the Japanese law" Japan itself recorded the American success. "Japan had broken its own code of selfish exclusiveness to obey the universal law of hospitality."

But Perry, just to show how little he thought of the Japanese orders to depart, ordered the entire squadron to get under way, not to leave but to go higher up the bay. The Commodore was determined to examine the channels toward Edo, sure that the show of force in carrying on surveys so close to the capital would make the government give more favorable consideration to the President's letter. The steamers moved into position with the two sloops-of-war, *Plymouth* and *Saratoga,* and the four ships started in a line abreast, each taking soundings of the water up the bay. The course was toward the shore, opposite the promontory of Uraga. The new ships' anchorage, which had been surveyed beforehand, was named the American Anchorage; it was about ten miles from Uraga, a mile and a half from shore, in thirteen fathoms of water. As soon as the ships were anchored, surveying parties were sent out again.

The Japanese officials came rushing to the flagship to inquire why the ships had sailed up the bay. They were informed that the move had been made to obtain a more secure anchorage, that Uraga was unsatisfactory because the water was rough and occasionally the winds blew with great force. The Japanese stated that the Americans had entered waters which had always been respected by strangers and that the squadron must not go any farther. They were answered that it was unreasonable to oppose a safe anchorage for visiting ships. In the United States foreigners were given every facility, and the Japanese would find the navigable waters free to them, too.

The next day, Perry transferred his commodore's pennant from the *Susquehanna* to the *Mississippi,* in which he proceeded up the bay some ten miles nearer Edo. He came close enough to see distinctly the port of Edo, which was on the southern side of the capital, but the city itself, made up mostly of low houses, was hidden behind a promontory. At that point, about ten miles from Edo, Perry turned back, even though he believed he could have come closer. He was a little fearful that too much alarm might hurt rather than help the reception of the President's letter, which was probably under consideration at that moment.

Perry had carefully considered the advantages of permitting Japan some time to consider the United States proposals. Accepting them meant, he knew, overturning some of the oldest laws of the empire. This would take time and deliberation, and he felt it inadvisable to wait for a reply. There were a few other very practical reasons. His supplies were running low and would not last more than another month. If he were forced to leave under such circumstances, he would have lost his advantage and been made to depart without a reply, which the Japanese would have taken as a triumph. He was happy to have an excuse to wait until the following spring for the answer from the Japanese government.

There was still another reason: none of the gifts from the

United States Government to the government and officials of Japan had arrived. It was essential to have these presents on hand if a favorable response to the President's letter was presented.

On Sunday morning, July 17, the squadron therefore left its anchorage, with the steamer *Susquehanna* towing the *Saratoga* and the *Mississippi* towing the *Plymouth*. The four vessels began their voyage without a yard of canvas set. The morning was fine as the four ships moved off in a regular line. Crowds gathered along the shore to watch the unfamiliar sight of the steam vessels. Many others crowded into boats and came in for a closer view.

Lofty Mount Fuji appeared and was passed. The ships set their course south. The next day the wind began blowing with such force that the two sloops-of-war had to be cast off. The wind grew to gale proportions and continued until the third day, when Perry headed for Okinawa.

The first visit of Commodore Perry and the American squadron to Edo Bay created a situation of impossible choices for the Shogunate. In Japan the prevailing opinion was to keep the ports closed to all Westerners but the Dutch at Nagasaki. But the Shogun's government, the Bakufu, and particularly his inner council of advisers, the Rōjū, knew that the defense of Japanese ports was pitifully inadequate. They knew also that the Americans were quite aware of this fact. In addition, the Shogun's government was in financial trouble. It had little money for more modern armaments even if they were available. Lastly, the Shogunate was especially vulnerable because Edo depended for its food supply on the seaborne movement of countless boats. The port could very easily be blockaded and the city starved.

The Bakufu was inclined to stall for time. Ieyoshi, the ruling Shogun, was so ill when Perry steamed up the bay that the news of the arrival of the Americans was not told him until a few days before the fleet left. He died before the end of July, but his death was not made known to the landed lords for a while. The following month, in an effort to win the widest national support, the Rōjū distributed copies of President Fillmore's letter to all the *daimyō*. For the first time in two hundred and fifty years, the vassals of a Tokugawa Shogun were being asked to express their opinion.

The appearance of the American warships in Edo Bay had been a severe shock to the Japanese noblemen in the Shogun's capital. In the past demanding foreigners had been concentrated around Nagasaki in the south and west, or around Hakodate in the north, affecting the rest of the country very little. Now, within a day's march of Edo itself, lay the black hulls of a powerful foreign fleet, commanded by an American who would not go away, but instead insisted on some agreement between the two countries. There were questions in the minds of the Japanese. Were they to be ordered around in their own waters? What right did a strange nation have to attempt forcing them into a commerce they did not want? What sort of friendship was being offered at cannon point?

Japanese historians have left records of the events inside Japan as the Perry fleet rode at anchor off Uraga. Everywhere there was the cry, "Jōi! Jōi! Expel the barbarians!" Alarm bells rang throughout the country, riders and couriers sped from castle to castle, spreading the ominous news. Ancient armor was dragged out of dusty caskets; spears and swords torn from their racks. Night and day the anvils rang as new weapons of war were being forged. Additional cannon were struck from the temple bells of Buddhist monasteries to fortify the principal points of defense. In the temples, Buddhist priests prayed to the gods of war. In their shrines, Shinto priests fasted while they called on the spirits of sea and storm to annihilate the invaders.

For the first time in seven centuries the head of the Shogun's council, Masahiro Abe, sent an envoy to the Emperor to consult about a matter of state. For their part, the Shogun's followers, having been given the opportunity to deliberate about the foreign policy of Japan, found themselves discussing many other problems besides the demands of the Americans. The discussions went on with much greater freedom than had been expected. The real American objective was assumed to be the conquest of Japan. Foreign trade, it was believed, would ruin the national economy.

Fifty replies came from the *daimyō*: thirty-four called for the rejection of the idea of opening Japanese ports to international trade; fourteen were indefinite but advocated a conciliatory approach; two urged an end to the policy of national isolation. Of the total, only eight demanded military action.

One of the firebrands was Keiei Matsudaira, a twenty-five-year-old *daimyō* from a branch of the Tokugawa house. He was vehement in his call for immediate preparation for war:

"The Bakufu having sent me Japanese translations of the two letters presented by the American ships which came recently to Uraga and instructed me to consider carefully the question of whether or no we should permit trade, taking into account all the advantages and disadvantages of so doing as well as the possible future repercussions, and then to report my views in full, I accordingly submit below a statement of my views.

"The President's letter, in contravention of the strict [se-

Dragonlike steamships and the kind of foreigners they bring
(The Mariners Museum, Newport News, Va.)

水師提督 名 ゴワラクセヘベルリ
年六十歳位

祝筒袖花色羅紗ノ羽丹
帽子黑幸紅白鳥毛ノカサリアリ
腕ニ金ノ環三ツアル 太刀金拵、其外金貝金
金ノ總數故不知

通詞役 名 クルフセシステン
黑羅紗
筒袖ノ
半臂
其余同シ
金・環ナシ

測量役
裝束
萌黄色
其余右ニ同シ

海中ニ栞案ヲナシ見セシ

鐵炮役
裝束
測量役ニ同シ

樂人
緋羅紗
裝束
白股引

水主 俗ニ黒坊ト云
帆桂ニ上リ
又ハ海中ニ
入役ナリ

但シ、黒人ヲ図ルニ

clusion] system we have maintained for over two hundred years, makes a number of impossible requests. What is more, there are passages in the letter presented by Perry, such as those in which he threatens the use of force to attain the objects of his mission and refers to our national laws as an unenlightened form of government, which are truly outrageous and show the utmost contempt for our country. They are such as to arouse extreme anger, and make it absolutely essential, I believe, for us to demonstrate our martial vigour to the whole world by completely destroying his ships.

"However, careful study of the present situation reveals that we are in fact helpless and cannot handle matters in that way. I believe that we have never been presented with a more difficult situation, that this is a national crisis more serious than any we have faced since the dawn of our history.

"For the Bakufu to grant the foreign request in its present form would, it is needless to say, disgrace our martial repute. Moreover, if other countries heard reports of it and all made similar requests, we would, by using up our limited resources in trade to satisfy the insatiable greed of the foreigners, bring daily nearer the collapse of our country. One might think, then, that we should pursue a policy of expediency, namely to grant their request while setting a three- to five-year limit [on the agreement], thus for a time warding off their insistence and leaving ourselves free to withdraw permission once our defences are completed, which would enable us to hold up our heads once again. This would [at first sight] seem the most appropriate action at this time. On the other hand, the Bakufu made no special preparations by way of strengthening our defences, despite the fact that ever since last year there had been frequent reports that the foreigners would come this summer, and even had to make up its mind about accepting the letters as a last-minute decision; and while this, too, was described as a policy of expediency, men of perception feel it to have been most reprehensible. Thus should the Bakufu decide, again in the name of expediency, to conclude treaties of friendship with foreigners, it would give the appearance of having fallen into the foreigners' toils simply from fear of their military might. Should this happen, I believe, our superb national morale would decline; and when we reached the end of the term of years [set for the agreement], there would not be the slightest hope of being quickly able to raise that morale again.

"There is a possibility that the foreigners would readily depart if the Bakufu were to grant their requests. But they have completed a survey of Edo Bay and have learned that there is nothing they need fear in our defences, especially at the Uraga entrance. This naturally increases their greed, and it is possible that when they come again they may resort to all kinds of violent action without even waiting for the Bakufu reply. Again, realizing that our defence preparations are being steadily effected, they may, even though the Bakufu grants their requests, decide to open hostilities while those preparations are still incomplete, indulging in acts of violence . . . and making such outrageous demands as for the right to swagger about in our capital or to open trading establishments. If they did this it is clear that even though the Bakufu issued orders for their lenient treatment, conflicts would occur and would lead to the opening of hostilities, for . . . our people . . . could not endure such things with patience.

"Then again, for the Bakufu to grant trade to all countries, even for a limited term of years, would be to humble itself before all countries. It would be the height of disgrace. And when the time came to withdraw permission, I believe, we would find ourselves the object of simultaneous attack by many powerful enemies. This would make it all the more impossible to conduct a successful defence. When it was realized that military weakness forced us to endure such disgrace, I very much fear that it would not only be in foreign countries that men might question the competence of our rulers, even the *daimyō* and lesser lords throughout the country. It might even be that Bakufu control of Japan would become ineffective, as happened at the end of the Ashikaga period.

"All this being so, I believe that the Bakufu's policy must be to refuse its consent for any of these concessions. However, I also believe that if the Bakufu does not grant the foreign demands war will break out and that the Bakufu cannot therefore refuse unless it is resolved to fight no matter how many warships are sent against us. Accordingly it is my belief that the greatest and most urgent task of the moment is for the Bakufu to notify the lords of all ranks in all provinces that the American requests are unacceptable and will be refused and that they are therefore to make preparations in anticipation of an outbreak of war when the Americans return next spring; for the Bakufu itself to undertake studies of defence technique and to unite opinion throughout the country; and for the early appointment of a supreme commander entrusted with complete authority in military affairs. . . .

"By returning an answer that it is impossible to grant the [American] requests, except for that seeking kind treatment for castaways, the Bakufu would be rebuking the foreigners for their faults without arousing their anger. . . . This would be both a just and proper policy, as well as a firm one. By acting in this way the Bakufu would gradually break down their attitude of contempt and tacitly forestall their greedy designs. And only thus, I believe, can the military valour of our land be restored to its former glory and our unexampled fair name and our permanent independence be fully maintained. If, on the other hand, we should lap ourselves in the luxury of peace to which we have for so long been accustomed, content with idleness and taking no decision either for peace or for war; if the foreign ships should come again while we wasted time in indecision and the foreigners should come to realize our lack of preparedness as we resorted to a policy of makeshifts; and if they should then set aflame our capital with their shells and cut down our troops with their small-shot, then it is evident to me that almost nothing could prevent the total collapse of our country. The dead would pile mountain-high and the streets would be filled with the sound of weeping. The confusion would be immense. When that time came, even if the Bakufu ordered the feudal lords to undertake defence, as it did recently, no general plan of defence would exist and all would have to do what they could individually. Complete victory would be impossible. However many troops were summoned from the provinces, the brave soldiers would fall in vain under the fire of foreign guns. All this would be inescapable. And not only would it call forth all our pity and regret, but also it would lead to national collapse. In the end peace negotiations would be undertaken and our country might even become a colony, a very slave, of the foreigners. At the very thought I cannot contain my wrath and indignation. The prospect so disturbs me that I can neither eat nor sleep. And since it is my belief that the safety and even the existence of our country are now at stake, I feel that the most urgent of all the urgent tasks of the present time is for the Bakufu to forbid all foolish talk of peace, to issue an immediate announcement that it is from this moment going to make plans for war, and to appoint a supreme commander. If a single day is wasted, then our defences are thereby one day delayed. I therefore ask with respect that the Bakufu may make its decision firmly and at once. . . ."

An older *daimyō*, named Nariakira Shimazu, expressed another point of view—delaying for time in order to build up Japan's military and naval strength and then to drive out the unwelcome foreigners:

"In accordance with Bakufu instructions, I have perused the Japanese translations of two letters recently presented by the American ships; and having been instructed that I must report my views without reserve on the problem of whether or no trade is to be permitted, this being a matter of the greatest national consequence, I comply herewith.

"We were given prior notice of the American request by the Dutch and it was often rumored by the foreigners then resident in Ryūkyū. It is no mere passing whim. For their part, too, they came and pressed their request despite full knowledge of the Shōgun's prohibition [of foreign intercourse]. Thus even if we decide to return a reply in accordance with our national laws it is unlikely that they will readily accept it. On the other hand, I do not believe we have any chance of victory if we try to expel them, for our defences are inadequate. Even if we succeeded in expelling them at the start, we know that they have ships that can traverse the seas at will and in particular that they have of recent days based many ships on China and the uninhabited islands [probably the Bonin Islands], with the result that they can at any time interrupt our sea communications. I therefore believe that what the Bakufu does on the present occasion will indeed prove to be of the greatest consequence.

"If the Bakufu grants the requests on this occasion its prestige will be dimmed and it will have broken faith with the King of Holland. Then again, I believe, if foreign countries get the idea that the Bakufu will grant their requests under threat of war, this will cause us great and constant difficulties for the future. I believe, then, that it might be inadvisable for the Bakufu to grant these present requests. However, if the Bakufu gives a blunt refusal when they come back next year, the foreigners might open hostilities. It is my belief, therefore, that the Bakufu should act so as to gain as much time as possible, explaining [to the Americans] that circumstances leave it no choice but to order them to return home, and should use the interval [so gained] to order completion of our coast defences. I think the Bakufu policy should be to seek to obtain some three years' grace, which should be ample. If we succeed in this, it is certain that by the time three years have passed all the provinces will have completed their preparations. When we have completed our military preparations, I believe, there will be ample means to obtain victory if the Bakufu orders expulsion, for Japan's military spirit has always been heroic.

". . . It is said that Japan's military valour is already held in respect by foreign countries and I therefore doubt whether the foreigners will act in an insulting manner once the Bakufu has made rigorous military preparations. Once we have constructed ample warships, even if the foreigners try to interrupt our sea communications the Bakufu will be able to take the necessary action; hence I think it might be best for the Bakufu to order expulsion as soon as this has been done [and not before]. . . .

"What I have written above is indeed temerity on my part, but it is a statement of my views made without reserve and without thought of consequences.

"Forwarded with respect.

"(*Note.* I think it would be even more dangerous for the Bakufu to give permission for the establishment of coaling stations and the other matters.)"

One of the two Japanese feudal lords who advocated the end of national isolation and the opening of the country was Toda Izu-no-kami, who had been a corecipient of President Fillmore's letter. The other was Naosuke Ii, who in five years was to become the Great Councilor of the Shogunate. His report to the Bakufu read:

"Before the year 1635 there were nine government-licensed

Labeled "true portraits" of Adams (left) and Perry, these sketches represented the widespread Japanese idea of a Westerner. (Black Ship Scroll: Honolulu Academy of Arts)

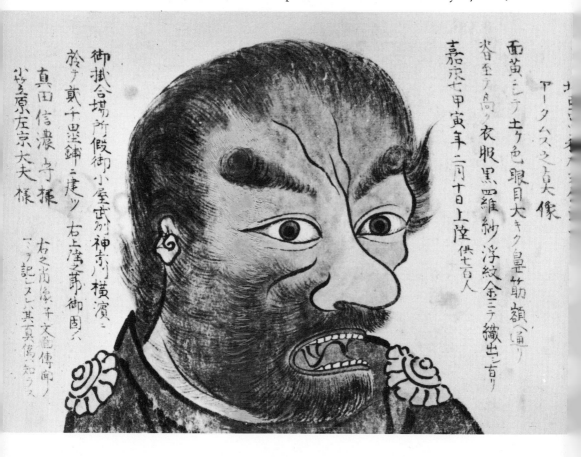

trading vessels belonging to Nagasaki, Sakai, Kyōto, &c., but with the prohibition of Christianity in the time of the Shōgun Iemitsu the Bakufu put an end to the voyages of these nine ships and laid down laws closing the country. Commerce was entirely limited to the Dutch and Chinese, no others being allowed to participate in it. Careful consideration of conditions as they are today, however, leads me to believe that despite the constant differences and debates into which men of patriotism and foresight have been led in recent years by their perception of the danger of foreign aggression, it is im-

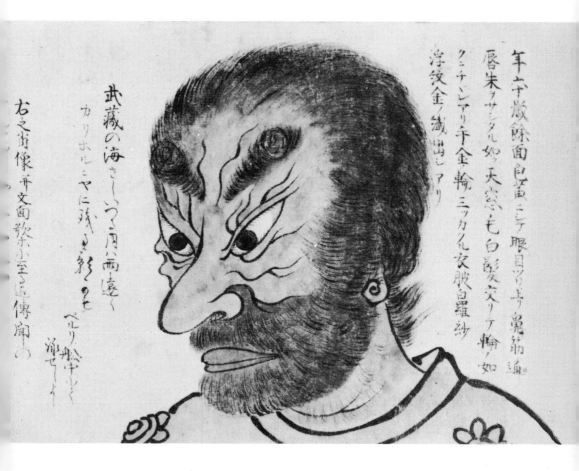

possible in the crisis we now face to ensure the safety and tranquillity of our country merely by an insistence on the seclusion laws as we did in former times. Moreover, time is essential if we are to complete our coast defences. Since 1609, when warships of over 500 *koku* [approximately five bushels] were forbidden, we have had no warships capable of opposing foreign attack on our coasts with heavy guns. Thus I am much afraid that were the foreigners now to seize as bases such outlying islands as Hachijō-jima and Ōshima, it would be impossible for us to remain inactive, though without warships we should have no effective means of driving them off. There is a saying that when one is besieged in a castle, to raise the drawbridge is to imprison oneself and make it impossible to hold out indefinitely; and again, that when opposing forces face each other across a river, victory is obtained by that which crosses the river and attacks. It seems clear throughout history that he who takes action is in a position to advance, while he who remains inactive must retreat. Even though the Shōgun's ancestors set up seclusion laws, they left the Dutch and the Chinese to act as a bridge [to the outside world]. Might this bridge not now be of advantage to us in handling foreign affairs, providing us with the means whereby we may for a time avert the outbreak of hostilities and then, after some time has elapsed, gain a complete victory?

"I understand that the coal for which the Americans have expressed a desire is to be found in quantity in Kyūshū. We should first tell them, as a matter of expediency, that we also have need of coal, but that should their need of it arise urgently and unexpectedly during a voyage, they may ask for coal at Nagasaki and if we have any to spare we will provide it. Nor will we grudge them wood and water. As for foodstuffs, the supply varies from province to province, but we can agree to provide food for the shipwrecked and unfortunate. Again, we can tell them, of recent years we have treated kindly those wrecked on our coasts and have sent them all home. There is no need for further discussion of this subject, and all requests concerning it should be made through the Dutch. Then, too, there is the question of trade. Although there is a national prohibition of it, conditions are not the same as they were. The exchange of goods is a universal practice. This we should explain to the spirits of our ancestors. And we should then tell the foreigners that we mean in future to send trading vessels to the Dutch company's factory at Batavia to engage in trade; that we will allocate some of our trading goods to America, some to Russia, and so on, using the Dutch to trade for us as our agents; but that there will be a delay of one or two years because we must [first] construct new ships for these voyages. By replying in this way we will take the Americans by surprise in offering to treat them generally in the same way as the Dutch.

"We must revive the licensed trading vessels that existed before the Kanei period [1624–44], ordering the rich merchants of such places as Ōsaka, Hyōgo, and Sakai to take shares in the enterprise. We must construct new steamships, especially powerful warships, and these we will load with goods not needed in Japan. For a time we will have to employ Dutchmen as masters and mariners, but we will put on board with them Japanese of ability and integrity who must study the use of large guns, the handling of ships, and the rules of navigation. Openly these will be called merchant vessels, but they will in fact have the secret purpose of training a navy. As we increase the number of ships and our mastery of technique, Japanese will be able to sail the oceans freely and gain direct knowledge of conditions abroad without relying on the secret reports of the Dutch. Thus we will eventually complete the organization of a navy. Moreover, we must shake off the panic and apprehensions that have beset us and abandon our habits of luxury and wasteful spending. Our defences thus strengthened, and all being arranged at home, we can act so as to make our courage and prestige resound beyond the seas. By so doing, we will not in the future be imprisoning ourselves; indeed, we will be able, I believe, so to accomplish matters at home and abroad as to achieve national security. Forestalling the foreigners in this way, I believe, is the best method of ensuring that the Bakufu will at some future time find opportunity to reimpose its ban and forbid foreigners to come to Japan, as was done in the Kanei period. Moreover, it would make possible the strictest prohibition of Christianity. And since I understand that the Americans and Russians themselves have only recently become skilled in navigation, I do not see how the people of our country, who are clever and quick-witted, should prove inferior to Westerners if we begin training at once.

"The national situation being what it is, if the Bakufu protects our coasts peacefully without bringing upon us permanent foreign difficulties, then even if that entails complete or partial change in the laws of our ancestors I do not believe such action could really be regarded as contrary to the wishes of those ancestors. However, I think it is essential to win the support of the country for Bakufu policy on this occasion, so the Bakufu should first notify the [Imperial] Court and then arrange to send Imperial messengers to the Ise, Iwashimizu, and Kashima shrines and a Tokugawa messenger to Nikkō, announcing there its resolve to secure tranquillity at home and security for the country. Trust in the will of the gods, after all, is the ancient custom of our land; and I believe, moreover, that by so doing the Bakufu may be able to unite national opinion.

"It is now no easy matter, by means of orders concerning the defence of the capital and the nearby coast, to ensure that all will be fully prepared for any sudden emergency, so not a moment must be wasted. However many iron walls we construct, they will certainly not be as effective as unity of mind if the unforeseen happens. The urgent task of the moment, therefore, is for the Bakufu to resolve on relieving the nation's anxieties and issue the appropriate orders.

"I am conscious of my temerity in putting forward views that conflict with the existing [seclusion] laws, but I have so reported in accordance with your orders that I was to do so fully and without reserve."

While the debate raged inside Japan, Commodore Perry made his way back to Hong Kong, stopping briefly at Okinawa. In August and September the steamer *Powhatan,* the sloop *Vandalia* and the store ship *Southampton* arrived from the United States to add to his command. By the end of the year the *Lexington,* a slow corvette, arrived with a miniature train and cars, a printing press, telegraph and other gifts for the Japanese. Perry's squadron was complete for a second trip to Japan.

3. COMMODORE PERRY:

THE TREATY OF KANAGAWA

*American sailors hunting and fishing in Japan; at left,
measuring the tide (Black Ship Scroll: Honolulu Academy
of Arts)*

P erry had planned, as he told the Japanese on his first visit, to return in April or May of 1854 to receive the reply to President Fillmore's letter. But toward the end of 1853 disturbing rumors reached him of suspicious movements of Russian and French warships. These nations might possibly be trying to beat the United States to an agreement with the Japanese. Consequently, in January of 1854, with the wintry seas still plagued by gales, fogs and similar dangers, Perry sailed from Hong Kong on the *Susquehanna*. With him went the *Powhatan* and the *Mississippi*, towing the *Lexington* and the *Southampton*. At Okinawa the squadron was joined by the *Macedonian,* the *Supply* and the *Vandalia*. The *Plymouth* and the *Saratoga* were on the way.

Word had been passed to Perry both from Russian and Dutch sources that the "Emperor," in this case referring to the Shogun, Ieyoshi, had died since receiving the American President's letter and that the government of Japan would prefer it if Perry's visit were postponed. The Commodore was not inclined to believe the report, suspecting some trick on the part of his informants. He also argued that he would deal with the new "Emperor" if indeed the report were true. Without further delay, he headed toward Japan and the forbidden bay of Edo.

Perry had left Japan on a Sunday and he returned on a Sunday, February 12, 1854, a bright, clear day but cold and penetrating. The wind the day before had forced his ships to drift considerably and daylight found them at the entrance to the wrong bay, where two other ships were seen closer to shore. They turned out to be the *Macedonian* and the *Vandalia,* which signaled to the flagship that the *Macedonian* had been grounded on a reef during the thick fog of the previous night. That afternoon, with the sea calmer, the *Mississippi* pulled the stranded ship off the reef, losing one hawser in the undertaking. Commodore Perry noted in his journal that the ledge of rocks had, of course, not been laid down on the imperfect chart copied from the Japanese. The captain of the *Macedonian*, Perry curtly noted, "ought not to have depended on it."

The commander of the *Mississippi* had a clerk, J. W. Spalding, who recorded the fleet's experiences seen from lower in the ranks. At daybreak the next morning, young Spalding had a chance to see Mount Fuji again; it towered over the countryside, the moon setting on one side, the rising sun burnishing the other "with brilliant glory." "No sight could have exceeded in magnificence the one presented by Foogee Yama," was his description of its appearance as the squadron entered the bay of Edo.

The *Susquehanna* had the *Vandalia* in tow; the *Powhatan* had the *Lexington*; and the *Mississippi*, because of its greater towing power, was pulling the *Macedonian*. As the year before, all ships' batteries were ready, the guns were loaded with shot, but Spalding felt a decided difference. "Instead of proceeding cautiously, as on the occasion of our former visit, the line of ships ran directly past their forts and into their inner bay, not stopping until reaching what had been called 'American Anchorage' on our first reconnaissance, about ten miles above the port of Uraga."

The ships had scarcely dropped their anchors before some Japanese officials came out to the flagship. They were received by Captain Adams, the Chinese interpreter, S. Wells Williams, the Dutch interpreter, Antón Portman and the Commodore's son, Oliver Hazard Perry, who was acting as secretary to his father.

To the Americans' delighted surprise, it was learned that

*Japanese sketches of Oliver Hazard Perry II, Antón Portman,
S. Wells Williams, Commander Henry A. Adams
(Namban Museum, Kobe)*

the Japanese government seemed ready to agree to some of
the requests in President Fillmore's letter and that a reception house had been prepared in Uraga, where high Japanese
officials would receive the Commodore. Perry refused to move
the squadron back ten miles to Uraga, which he had declared
unsatisfactory as an anchorage. He said he would move closer
to Edo if his present position did not suit the Japanese.

The Commodore sent word that he would consent to a
meeting opposite the ships' present anchorage, but the Japanese countered with another suggestion: that the meeting take
place at Kamakura, about twenty miles below Uraga, not far
from the place where the *Macedonian* had run aground. The
Commodore turned down the suggestion with finality. The
Japanese returned to their argument that Uraga had been
designated by Imperial decree and the rule could not be

changed. To Perry it sounded like "an apparent ultimatum." Perry's countersuggestion that he would go up to the capital itself was confronted by the direct warning, "You cannot be received at Edo." These exchanges went on for several days, while American surveying boats continued to chart the waters of the bay. The operation was protested by the Japanese, but the American commander refused to call in his boats.

The seamen on board the American ships, according to Spalding, learned that the news of the Shogun's death was true, but in the official dealings between the officers references were more oblique. Captain Adams alluded to the report of of the death of the Emperor, saying he had heard a high dignitary had died.

The Japanese answered, "Yes, a very high man died lately."

"What was his rank?" asked Adams.

"He was a prince," replied the Japanese official.

This example was used to show that Perry felt it "a matter of the greatest difficulty to get at the truth, the Japanese being as indirect and evasive as possible in regard to the simplest matter of fact." It may be that the Japanese did not want to emphasize that the Emperor and the Shogun were not the same persons and that the President's letter had been accepted by the Shogun, to whom it was not officially addressed.

A few days after Perry's arrival, the official Japanese delegation appeared in Uraga. It was headed by Noboru Hayashi, Lord Rector of the University, who was to act as chief negotiator for the Shogunate. Kurakawa Kahei, chief of the local officials, was immediately dispatched to tell the Commodore that the delegation had come from Edo and that the meeting place was ready at Uraga. Hayashi kept a diary of the negotiations. His first entry, for the twentieth day of the first month—February 18—recorded the American response:

"Perry had replied that he was resolved to go to Yedo and

discuss matters at length with members of the Grand Council and refused to return [to Uraga]. Perry was said to be ill and did not meet the officials, but sent his replies by Adams."

That day Perry transferred his pennant to the *Powhatan,* which became his flagship. Perry's message, communicated by Captain Adams, read:

"The Commodore expects to be received at Yedo, agreeably to the customs of all countries.

"In consideration of the size of our ships, and their great value, he cannot return to the anchorage at Uraga, nor even remain at this place much longer, but will have to go higher up in the bay towards Yedo, where the vessels can be more secure.

"If the great man (chief commissioner) will appoint an officer of proper rank to meet Captain Adams on shore, near where the ships are now lying, to determine when and where the interview with the Commodore shall take place, he must let us know by noon of Tuesday next.

"The Commodore will be happy to place a ship at the disposal of the great man, to bring him up to the place of interview, and take him back to Uraga, if he wishes it.

"When the officer comes to meet Captain Adams, he had better bring a letter to show that he has proper authority, and a person must be sent to conduct Captain Adams to the place of meeting."

The response of the Japanese high commissioners, addressed to the Commodore and written in Japanese and Dutch, restated their instructions:

"We are compelled by the order of the Emperor to meet the ambassador of the President of the United States of America either at Kamakura or Uraga.

"In the interim we shall talk about the negotiations of commerce and the influence it must exercise upon the well-being of the Japanese and American nations. It is out of the question now. This is all according to truth."

Perry insisted that "his instructions are to receive the answer to the President's letter at Yedo." Nevertheless he consented to send Captain Adams and the *Vandalia* to Uraga, where they arrived on February 22, Washington's Birthday. Adams was dissatisfied with the buildings there, which he found badly sited, poorly constructed and too limited in size. In his diary, the Lord Rector described the visit. The commissioners arrived at the reception hall, but Hayashi and another dignitary were determined not to present themselves unless the Commodore himself put in an appearance.

"Adams presented his card, which was inscribed with European letters, and each of our officials returned his card upon which was written his title. (At this moment Mimasaka-no-kami [Mayayoshi Izawa] folded his fan with a sharp report. The foreigners were much alarmed and their expressions changed; they placed their hands on the pistols which they wore at their waist and assumed a resolute attitude; but when Mimasaka-no-kami leisurely drew out his spectacles and began slowly to examine the cards one by one, they noticed his lack of concern and appeared to be relieved of their anxiety.) Adams presented a letter in Chinese, the contents of which he did not discuss. He said that when the Envoy landed he would discuss it in detail. . . . (Tea, cakes and rice wine were now passed.) At the eighth hour, the foreigners withdrew. (This being the birthday of Washington, the founder of America, the salutes which they had refrained from firing were fired.)"

The American version of the reception was:

"The prince now entered, and his card was handed to Captain Adams, upon which was recorded his full name and title, thus: Hayashi-Daigaku-no-Kami, i.e., Hayashi, Lord of Daigaku."

At the American Anchorage, the squadron celebrated Washington's birthday with the usual salutes from all of the ships. Many of the Japanese came aboard the ships to see the cannons being fired. "The most intelligent among them had heard of the name of Washington," wrote the Commodore in his journal, "though they had very vague notions of his history or character."

While Adams was kept at Uraga for another day because of a severe storm in the harbor, Kayama suddenly presented himself. It had been feared that his conduct during the squadron's first visit had brought disgrace on him, or even that he had been condemned to the ceremonial Japanese suicide. Kayama excused his absence on the grounds of long illness.

Perry, having little hope that Adams could convince the Japanese commissioners to come up to meet him near his present anchorage, decided to act upon his threat and actually moved his squadron so close to Edo that the city could be seen from the masthead; the city bells, striking through the night, could clearly be heard. The squadron anchored off Kanagawa, just below Edo.

The Lord Rector of the University, on February 25, noted that the seven American ships had reached a point off the

lighthouse at Edo called Haneda. That day, he wrote, "an express arrived from Edo bearing official instructions, stating in effect that, as the arrival of the vessels at Edo would be regarded as due to the negligence of the Shogunate, the Envoy should be met at Kanagawa."

The following day the Lord Rector indicated the real position of Eizaemon Kayama, who was still being accepted by the Americans as the Governor of Uraga.

"The police officer, Kayama Eizaemon, was sent out to the foreign vessels. He said, 'As there are some good sites near Kanagawa, how would it be if one were selected and the negotiations held there? How about Yokohama?'"

The change of attitude by the Japanese was explained by Perry:

"Finding that the Commodore was immovable in purpose and evidently inclined to approach nearer to Yedo, [Kayama] suddenly abandoned the previously pretended ultimatum of the Japanese commissioners as to the place of meeting.

"Thus after having interposed for the last ten days all possible objections to the squadron's moving farther up the bay, and having used every inducement to prevail upon the Commodore to return to Uraga, they suddenly abandoned the position from which they had so frequently declared they could not possibly be moved. They had discovered that the

*The arrival of Commodore Perry; six-panel screen
(Historiographical Institute, Tokyo University;
P: International Society for Educational Information, Tokyo)*

Commodore was not to be shaken from his resolution, and, finding that the ships had already approached within eight miles of their capital, they thought it politic to stop them there, while it was practicable, by a conciliatory concession."

The report from Captains Buchanan and Adams was favorable concerning the spot at Kanagawa (Yokohama). It had a safe and ample anchorage a mile distant from shore, with abundant space both for landing and exhibiting the presents intended for the Emperor. Perry concurred in the choice. The American ships moved in closer to shore and formed an anchorage in a line that put five miles of the beach within range of their guns.

While the buildings were being erected with what Spalding called "Babel-like activity," visits were paid to the American ships by some of the lesser Japanese officials. Kayama was given a dinner on the *Susquehanna,* together with ten others. At first they found difficulties with the knives and forks instead of their accustomed chopsticks; they drank wine from the larger American goblets as though they were tiny sake cups, drinking toasts with gusto. During the two-hour repast, one of the Japanese sang a song which Spalding described as "a kind of cross between the half wail, half-vocal screech of the Chinese, a boy dragging a stick over the palings and a severe asthma." In return, an American sang a song called "Ginger Blue"—which surprised and delighted the young commander's clerk with the impertinence "to indulge in such refrains before the potentate presence that once required knocking head from a Russian count!"

During the dinner, the Japanese had laid aside their swords and Spalding had a chance to examine them. He was amazed at the temper of their steel, the razor-sharpness of their blades, the surfaces "so highly polished that they seemed black in-

日本通詞
マトウ

The only Japanese member of the American squadron, possibly Sam Patch (Black Ship Scroll: Honolulu Academy of Arts)

stead of bright and the breath disappears as from the face of the finest mirror."

The Japanese interpreters now included one who spoke English tolerably well. He said he had learned it from an American at Nagasaki, but he did not tell Spalding that this American was one who had been imprisoned there and liberated by the *Preble* in 1849. He was Enosuke Moriyama, who had learned his English from Ranald MacDonald, the adventurous seaman who had deliberately stranded himself in Japan in 1848.

During this time Kayama was handed a letter written by a Japanese attached to the American squadron, who was called

Sam Patch by the sailors. He was a crewman of the Japanese ship which had been driven by a storm off the coast of Japan and been brought to San Francisco. Joseph Heco had returned to the United States, and fearing for their lives, all but Patch had preferred to remain in China. A few days later Kayama encountered his castaway countryman, who fell on his knees in terror. Sam elected to stay with the squadron in spite of promises of full safety if he returned.

The Japanese visitors were eager to acquire English dictionaries and grammars. Offered a trip to the United States, they said they would wait until they could come in their own ships.

Meanwhile the houses on shore were rapidly rising. As agreed, there was no enclosure. The Japanese said that since they now knew the Americans better, there would be no soldiers at the Reception Hall. In return, Perry assured Kayama that he would be accompanied only by a guard of honor to celebrate the occasion.

On March 4 the *Saratoga* arrived and anchored in line with the squadron. It had encountered severe weather and welcomed a safe anchorage. Its arrival at Kanagawa was duly entered in Hayashi's diary, which noted the "total of eight ships." The next day the report to the Japanese commissioners was: "Perry said that he would enter into negotiations, but if his proposals were rejected, he was prepared to make war at once; that in the event of war he would have 50 ships in nearby waters and 50 more in California, and that if he sent word he could summon a command of one hundred warships within twenty days."

Two days later a Marine on the *Mississippi* named Robert Williams died of an affliction of the brain.

March 8 was the day appointed for the Commodore to go ashore. The treaty house was adorned with streamers and gay hangings. The entrance was flanked by long oblong banners of white cotton with a bright red stripe across the center. The site had been fenced in by an enclosure of screen cloths, making it seem like a stockade or prison. The screens were removed at Perry's insistence. Aboard the *Mississippi* there was very little excitement and suspense, except among some newcomers who had not been present at the first landing in July the year before. A year earlier there had been doubt and uncertainty, and the possibility had been strong that the Japanese might trap the Americans. The Japanese themselves were saying that at first they considered the Americans as enemies, now they were receiving them as friends. Besides, as Spalding wrote, the Americans knew exactly the state of Japanese defenses, and the squadron was three times as strong.

The second American landing in Japan was prepared to be as much of a show as possible. All marines who could be spared from duty were ordered to appear in full uniform, and all officers and sailors who could be made available were detailed to add to the spectacle. The officers were in undress uniform, frock coats, caps and epaulets, equipped with swords and pistols. The sailors, dressed in blue jackets and white frocks, carried muskets and cutlasses and wore pistols. The company, consisting of about five hundred men, embarked in twenty-seven boats, under the command of Commander Buchanan, and, forming a line abreast, rowed to shore in order. There they were arranged in two divisions on either side of the landing, their bows pointing away from the shore.

Soon after, with a salute of seventeen guns from the *Macedonian,* Commodore Perry stepped from his flagship, the *Powhatan,* into a white barge and was rowed to the beach. The Americans fell into line behind Perry, and, accompanied by the bands playing a lively tune, the procession moved up to

左右隊長官六人ツヽ
前後先防戦士数人
上陸之図
横濱
本牧
亜墨利加人
惣勢五百人

Landing of the Americans at Kanagawa, detail of a Japanese print (Library of Congress)

the treaty house. There a group of Japanese guards, in richly colored costumes, waited on either side of the entrances. As the Americans passed between these retainers, a large number of Japanese officials came out to greet them and conduct them into the building. Howitzers began firing a twenty-one gun "special ambassador" salute for the Japanese high commissioner, the Lord Rector of the University. The flag of the Tokugawa Shogunate, with its trefoil design—still supposed by the Americans to be the imperial banner—was hoisted to the masthead of the *Powhatan*.

The Commodore and his officers and interpreters had barely been seated on the left, the place of honor, when the five

Japanese commissioners entered the official hall. All the subordinate Japanese officials immediately prostrated themselves and remained on their knees.

The commissioners were august-looking figures to the Americans. Their manners were serious but courteous. They were dressed in rich flowing robes of silk. Hayashi, chief member of the commission, was about fifty-five, a man of handsome appearance, with both a brave expression and a benevolent look. Satohiro Ido, Tsushima-no-kami, was probably fifty years of age, tall but corpulent. The youngest, Mayayoshi Izawa, Mimasaka-no-kami, was about forty. He appeared quite lively, with a fondness for fun and a liking for music. Chōhei Udono, fourth member of the delegation, was a censor of the Bakufu, whose duty it was to keep watch on the others. A fifth commissioner, whose rank and title were a mystery, was listed by the Americans. He had been a last-minute addition to the Japanese delegation and his role was unclear. He sat somewhat apart from the other dignitaries, and at his feet sat a scribe who constantly took notes of everything that happened or was said. He acted as secretary to the chief commissioner. The Americans thought he was a spy.

After the exchange of civilities and the invariable tea in porcelain cups, the two delegations moved into a smaller inner chamber, accommodating about ten persons. The proceedings were then begun, with the delivery to Commodore Perry of a roll of paper, which proved to be an answer to President Fillmore's letter, delivered the previous July. It appeared to be presented in the name of the Japanese Emperor, though it actually was from the Shogunate:

"The return of your excellency, as ambassador of the United States to this Empire, has been expected according to the letter of his Majesty the President, which letter your excellency delivered last year to his Majesty the Emperor of this Empire.

"It is quite impossible to give satisfactory answers at once to all the proposals of your government, as it is most positively forbidden by the laws of our Imperial ancestors; but for us to continue attached to the ancient laws, seems to misunderstand the spirit of the age; however, we are governed now by imperative necessity.

"At the visit of your excellency last year to this Empire, his Majesty the former Emperor was sick, and is now dead. Subsequently, his Majesty the present Emperor [Iésada] ascended the throne; the many occupations in consequence thereof are not yet finished, and there is no time to settle other business thoroughly. Moreover, his Majesty the new Emperor, at the accession to the throne, promised to the princes and high officers of the Empire to observe the laws. It is therefore evident that he cannot now bring about any alteration in the ancient laws.

"Last autumn, at the departure of the Dutch ship, the superintendent of the Dutch trade in Japan was requested to inform your government of this event, and a reply in writing has been received.

"At Nagasaki arrived recently the Russian ambassador to communicate a wish of his government. He has since left the said place, because no answer would be given to any nation that might communicate similar wishes. However, we admit the urgency of, and shall entirely comply with, the proposals of your government concerning coal, wood, water, provisions, and the saving of ships and their crews in distress.

*Banquet for the Americans, given by Japanese
commissioners; sketch for painting by Hideki
(Namban Museum, Kobe)*

After being informed which harbor your excellency selects, that harbor shall be prepared, which preparation it is estimated will take about five years. Meanwhile a commencement can be made with the coal at Nagasaki by the next Japanese first month, (Siogoots) (16th of February, 1855).

"Having no precedent with respect to coal, we request your excellency to furnish us with an estimate, and upon due consideration this will be complied with, if not in opposition to our laws. What do you understand by provisions, and how much coal?

"Finally, anything ships may be in want of that can be furnished from the production of this Empire shall be supplied. The prices of merchandise and articles of barter to be fixed by Kurakawa Kahei and Moriyama Yenosuke [Enosuke]. After settling the points before mentioned, the treaty can be concluded and signed at the next interview.

"Seals attached by order of the high gentlemen.

"MORIYAMA YENOSUKE"

Perry requested that the document be signed by the high commissioner. The subject of a treaty, uppermost in Perry's mind, was immediately broached, and a draft was put into the hands of the Japanese. As a model to guide the deliberations, a copy of the treaty between the United States and China was also presented.

With these preliminaries over, Perry informed the Japanese commissioners that an American seaman had died two days before and he requested consent to buy a plot of land in which to bury the body, on an island down the bay marked on the squadron's charts as "Webster Island." There was some objection on the part of the Japanese, who wanted the burial to take place at Uraga, but Perry insisted. He said he was prepared to accomplish the interment of the dead sailor even against the wishes of the Japanese delegation.

The conference, including the subject of the American seaman's burial, was recorded in his diary by the chief Japanese delegate:

"*10th* [March 8]. . . . (Three sides of the Reception Hall, that is to say, the left, right and back, were guarded by retainers. . . . Off-shore there were several hundred guard boats). At the ninth hour the Envoy Perry came ashore. (There was a line of 28 barges, and on the Envoy's barge alone a white flag was hoisted. About 600 men in all came ashore and formed in line to the sound of music. Perry with more than 30 men entered the Reception Hall and took his seat. . . .)

"The Lord Rector: 'It is a great pleasure to make your acquaintance and to felicitate you on having completed a second voyage from distant parts.'

"Perry: 'I am glad to make your acquaintance. I felicitate you on your good health. On this occasion, I shall fire a salute of 21 guns in honor of the Princes and 18 guns in honor of the Lord Rector. Another salute of 18 guns will be fired to celebrate my first landing.' (After he explained the foreign custom of firing salutes of 21 guns for sovereigns, 18 guns for ministers of state, and 15 guns for those of next lower rank, upon auspicious occasions, the shots were fired in succession).

"The Lord Rector: 'Last summer, the President sent our Taicoon [Tycoon, or great man—another form of reference to the Shogun] a letter, which you presented. Among the various requests made in this letter, there were some referring to fuel, water and provisions. An order has already been issued regarding this matter. As you appear earnestly to desire coal, we will make an exception and supply you with what we have. Further, with regard to the kindly treatment of shipwrecked persons, we have had laws in the past regarding shipwrecked persons; but such persons will be treated with kindness hereafter. We will assent, therefore, to two of these proposals, but the others, regarding trade and so on, we cannot accept.'

"Perry (not replying to these statements): 'You must pardon me for bringing up this matter so abruptly, but a member of the crew of one of my ships, a man of low rank, has just died. If his death had occurred in any other country, he would have been buried without delay, but I understand that the laws of your country are particularly severe, and I wish, therefore, first to ask where he may be buried. After examining the shore, I observe that the island of Natsushima, which lies off Kanagawa, has upon it no houses or dwellings, and I assume, therefore, that there will be no objection to his burial there. If it should not cause you any inconvenience, I wish to consider his burial there to be a settled matter.' (At this moment, one of the barges, bearing a white flag, returned to Kanagawa from Uraga. It was beached on Natsushima, and four or five persons landed and walked about as though searching for a burial plot).

"The Lord Rector: 'It is indeed sad that one coming from so far a place should die. Even the life of one of humble rank is not a light matter. In Japan, we bury persons in temples and not in places where there are no human habitations. True, he was not one of our countrymen, but how disconsolate would be burial in this uninhabited place! We will select a place where he may be buried. Natsushima is an uninhabited island belonging to certain lords and nothing can be done . . . without the permission of the authorities. He should be buried at the foot of the Uraga Lighthouse.'

"Perry: 'Whether the remains can be sent to Uraga will depend upon the state of the weather, and will entail much

Funeral of the American Marine Robert Williams;
Japanese sketch (Namban Museum, Kobe)

trouble. I intend to remain here until the present negotiations are concluded, even if that should require one or two years. During this period, others will die; and it would be extremely inconvenient to remove the remains each time to Uraga. Dead men can do no wrong.'

"The Lord Rector: 'As foreign vessels are not permitted to enter the bay beyond Uraga, your countrymen will be unable in later years to worship at his grave; but if this is not a matter of importance to you, he may be buried in a temple nearby; and the grave may be removed later, if circumstances require this.' (This matter was raised unexpectedly, and we, as well as the foreigners, wished to settle it without delay. For this reason, a reply was made at once).

"Perry: 'I thank you very much. If you will agree to this

arrangement, it would be most convenient, on the understanding that the graves may be removed later, if necessary. The fact that our countrymen will be unable later to worship before these graves is not of importance, and I hope that you will accede to my request.' (Perry appeared to be extraordinarily grateful, to the extent even of shedding tears.)

" 'We have in our country always regarded human life as of the first importance in the conduct of our government, and, therefore, whenever any of our countrymen—of course—or persons belonging to another country or even to a country with which we do not ordinarily have intercourse, reach our shores after having been shipwrecked, we exert every effort to rescue them, and we treat them with kindness. I perceive no sign, however, that human life is counted in your country to be of great importance; for whenever a vessel of any foreign country approaches your shores, you repel it with guns; and when shipwrecked persons reach the shore, you treat them like slaves and keep them in harsh imprisonment. Whenever Japanese are shipwrecked off our shores, my countrymen rescue them and send them back to their own country; but when such persons return to their own country, you will not receive them. You thus seem to have no regard even for your own countrymen and to be exceedingly inhumane. Our country has become one of the great powers, despite various circumstances; our California faces Japan, the two being divided, not by another country, but by the Pacific Ocean. In a short time, the ships frequenting Japanese waters will greatly multiply in number, and if the government of your country continues to adhere to its harsh practices and a large number of lives are sacrificed, we would not overlook it. If your country should persist in its present practices and fail to mend them, and if ships are not helped, it will surely be looked upon with hostility. If your country becomes an enemy,

Americans surveying (Black Ship Scroll: Honolulu Academy of Arts)

we will exhaust our resources if necessary to wage war. We are fully prepared to engage in a struggle for victory. Our country has just had a war with a neighboring country, Mexico, and we even attacked and captured its capital. Circumstances may lead your country also into a similar plight. It would be well for you to reconsider.'

"The Lord Rector: 'If forced by circumstances, we also will go to war; but many of your statements are not true, due, I assume, to the fact that many of your ideas have been created by mistaken reports. It is only natural, perhaps that as we have no intercourse with other countries you should have mistaken ideas about our government. Our government is not the inhumane thing you describe. First, we excel any other country in the importance we attach to human life. For this reason, we have enjoyed peace for more than 300 years. If we were so inhumane as to consider human life cheaply, the state I have described could not have been possible. Our laws forbid the construction of large vessels and their navigation to foreign countries, so we cannot rescue vessels on the high seas; but when foreign vessels are in distress along our shores and ask for fuel, water, or provisions we have been accustomed to mete out kindly treatment. It is not true, as you said, that we do not help ships in distress wrecked along our coasts. We will continue to supply fuel, water and provisions. Then, your statement that shipwrecked persons have been thrown like slaves into prison, must be due to false reports. According to our laws, shipwrecked persons wherever they may be found, are to be treated with kindness and sent to Nagasaki and there delivered to the Dutch captain, by whom they are returned to their respective countries. Some time ago, certain of your countrymen arrived in distress at Matsumae [Ranald Mac-Donald and the crew of the *Lagoda*], which is a place in the north; they were all taken to Nagasaki and from there sent to your country. There are persons who, even though in distress, are not of good character: they violate our laws and do as they please. Such we are obliged to detain temporarily before sending them to Nagasaki; but it is the unlawful behavior of persons of this character which alone brings about such treat-ment. It is quite possible that upon their return, they assert that they were treated like slaves, and otherwise circulate false reports. There is nothing inhumane about our govern-ment; and I am certain that if you will examine the state of our country and study the facts, your doubts will be dissolved. If you in your country truly value human life, you will not allow the resentment of successive years to crystalize. These are not matters so grave as to make war necessary. It would be well for you indeed to reconsider.'

"Perry: 'I have heard that your country has issued an order

to supply foreign ships with fuel, water and provisions, and to rescue vessels in distress, as you have said; but our ships have frequently approached this country and have met with nothing but refusals; and they have not readily been able to obtain fuel and water. If your government is in fact as you describe it to be, and if you continue hereafter to supply fuel, water and provisions, and give help to those in distress, nothing more can be said. I desire, however, that a decree may be issued concerning the method by which you will hereafter supply fuel, water, provisions and coal. I shall be satisfied also if you reply to me that you will hereafter treat shipwrecked persons in as kindly a manner as you have just described.

" 'Why do you not allow commerce? Commerce has to do with the things which a nation has and with what it lacks; it is a source of great profit and now flourishes between the countries of the world day and night. It brings great wealth to each country. If you open your country to commerce it will bring you great profit and will surely be to your great advantage.'

"The Lord Rector: 'However much commerce has to do with what a nation has or lacks and would therefore be to its advantage, our country since the beginning has found the things which it produces to be sufficient for its own needs. We are not discontented at being without the products of other countries. Having decided that we shall not permit commerce, we cannot easily decide to permit it. You say that your principal purpose in coming was to have greater value placed on human life and to have help given to ships. You have attained your purpose. Now, commerce has to do with profits, but has it anything to do with human life? Is it not enough that you have gained what you sought?'

"Perry cogitated for some time and then said: 'You are

right. As you say, I came because I valued human life, and the important thing is that you will give our vessels help. Commerce brings profit to a country, but it does not concern human life. I shall not insist upon it.'

"Perry now drew out of one of his pockets a small book and then returned it. He repeated this two or three times, but finally he drew it out and said: 'This book is the treaty made between the United States and China when commerce was first established. I brought it because, if commerce were to be permitted, it would govern this matter fairly and equitably; but in view of your arguments, I shall not insist. Having brought it, I hope that you will peruse it for your information only.' (He presented a book in Chinese).

"The Lord Rector: 'We cannot easily agree to engage in commerce, as I said; but if you desire me merely to peruse your treaty with China, I have no objection to doing so.' He received the book. It now being the evening, the discussions were brought to an end, and the banquet was brought in. The Lord Rector withdrew to the retiring room in order to indicate that his rank is higher than that of Perry and also to enable him, in the interests of his country, to maintain an attitude of reserve. Tsushima-no-kami, Mimasaka-no-kami, Udono and Mantaro ate with the foreigners. As soon as the banquet ended, the Lord Rector entered to make his farewells. Perry and the other foreigners then returned."

The next day, March 9, a Japanese official came aboard the *Mississippi* to accompany the funeral party. As the funeral boats pushed off, all ships lowered their flags to half-mast. The body was buried at a very picturesque spot a short distance from Yokohama, with full rites of the Protestant Episcopal Church. The Japanese paid their respects to the dead stranger with a Buddhist ceremony.

The Monday following was set for the presentation of the

gifts which had been brought from America. The Japanese were very excited about the new American instruments and machines. They were particularly fascinated by the telegraph, which was set up with a mile of wire strung between two stations. They were shown its ability to send and receive messages in English, Japanese and Dutch. Not fully convinced at first, they tried racing the message with their fleetest runners, with inevitable victory to the telegraph. The tiny railroad delighted them. It was a perfect specimen of delicate workmanship but hardly big enough to carry a six-year-old child in comfort. Nevertheless, the Japanese would not be cheated out of a ride, so they sat themselves on the roof and many a dignified figure found himself whirling around the small circular track at twenty miles an hour, his robes flying in the wind.

The presents to the Shogun and his wife filled several large boats. The Americans thought the gifts were for the Emperor and Empress of Japan. Besides the one-quarter size Lilliputian railroad, complete with locomotive, tender, car and tracks, there were copper lifeboats, two sets of telegraph instruments and the daguerreotype, five rifles, three muskets, eighteen swords, one carbine and twenty pistols; nine volumes of James Audubon's *Birds of America;* clocks, a sheet-iron stove, assorted fine perfumery; wine and whiskey, cordials and champagne, charts, paper, seed and a large quantity of agricultural implements. For distribution to other dignitaries there were pistols, wines, chinaware, cherry cordials, books, scarlet broadcloth and the like.

For the Shogun's wife the list of gifts, according to Spalding's account, included a telescope, a lorgnette in a gilded case, a lady's toilet box; a scarlet velvet dress, a flowered silk dress, a robe, Audubon's illustrated works, a set of china, a mantelpiece clock, a parlor stove, wines, perfumes and soaps. Officially only three items were listed: a flowered silk em-

An American train, illustration from Manjiro Nakahama's account of his rescue. Nakahama was placed in charge of the Western gifts presented to Japan, which included a miniature railroad. His knowledge of English also led to his appointment as translator of Perry's documents during the negotiations; later he became interpreter to the first Japanese mission to the United States. (The Millicent Library, Fairhaven, Mass.)

broidered dress, a gilded toilet box, and six dozen assorted perfumery.

Books on history, architecture and geology were presented to the Japanese councillors, as well as a copy of Appleton's *Dictionary*. The presentation of a Webster's dictionary was very welcome to the interpreter; while other valued gifts were

Irish potatoes and even a hydraulic ram, Spalding wrote.

The day of the presentation of the gifts appeared less festive to the Lord Rector. He noted that Perry had not come ashore, nor had Commander Adams. The presentations were under the direction of Captains Abbott and Lee. "Whenever Perry and Adams went ashore, Abbott and Lee remained on their vessel, and whenever Abbott and Lee went ashore, Perry and Adams remained on their vessel. Abbott is said to be of the same rank as Perry and wears the same uniform, while Lee is of the same rank as Adams. Considering these facts, we assume that they plan, in the event of Perry and Adams landing and being captured by our soldiers lying in ambush, that Abbott, who would be afloat, should replace Perry as admiral of the fleet, while Lee should replace Adams."

Four days later the Lord Rector and his fellow commissioners returned to the conference house in a ceremonial barge, called the *Tenjin Maru,* which they used from that time on. They found Perry, Adams and Buchanan, attended by about two hundred men. The Japanese record of the meeting that day read:

"Perry: 'It was a great pleasure to have met you the other day. I am very glad that the presentation of gifts has been completed.'

At first the Japanese tried to outrun the telegraph messages.
(Brown University Library, Providence, R.I.:
Anne S. K. Brown Military Collection)

"The Lord Rector: 'It was indeed very courteous of you to have sent presents to us individually, as well as to the Shogun.' "

The conversation then turned to the supplying of fuel, water and provisions to American ships in distress, which the Japanese agreed to. The matter of payment was disposed of quickly, but the ports, where such supplies would be made available were not so easily decided. The Japanese proposed Nagasaki, which Perry flatly refused. He stated his objections to the humiliating treatment long experienced by the Dutch, which he said the Americans would never consent to. Perry objected also that Nagasaki was too far to the south and west to be of any advantage to a ship headed for Canton. It would be just as easy for a ship to reach China as Nagasaki.

Other ports were suggested by the Americans, for example, Kanagawa, where they were, but the Japanese just as emphatically rejected this proposal. Eventually the ports of Hakodate in the north and Shimoda near the mouth of Edo Bay were proposed, subject to examination and acceptance by the Americans.

On the twenty-fourth of the month, gifts from the Shogun were to be presented in public recognition of the generosity of the United States. That day the Commodore landed at Yokohama with his suite of officers and was received at the treaty house with the usual ceremonies. The rooms were filled with presents, which covered the settees, tables, stands and floor. The gifts consisted of rich brocades and silks, lacquerware, tables, trays and drinking cups, porcelains, fans, pipe cases and articles of apparel. The objects were carefully classified in accordance with the rank of those for whom they were intended. Perry was presented with two complete sets of Japanese coins, three matchlocks and two swords. The

American commodore was particularly gratified by the gift of the Japanese coins, which being in direct opposition to Japanese law, seemed a particular mark of friendship. One gift for the President of the United States was heaped on the beach. It was more than a hundred sacks of rice, ready to be loaded aboard the ships. It was then explained to the Americans that by Japanese custom, when royal gifts were bestowed they were accompanied by a certain quantity of rice.

Along with the mounds of rice there were seen twenty-five mountainous men, who, in the words of the *Narrative,* "tramped down the beach like so many elephants." The Americans were more horrified than delighted at this display of muscular power by these Sumo wrestlers. Perry found himself forced to examine one, reputed the bully of Edo, and he felt the giant's muscular bulk. "They were all so immense in flesh that they appeared to have lost their distinctive features, and seemed to be only twenty-five masses of fat. Their eyes were barely visible. Their heads were set almost directly on their bodies, with merely folds of flesh where the neck and chin are usually found. Their great size, however, was due more to the development of muscle than to fat, for, although they were well fed, they were not less well exercised and capable of great feats of strength."

The Lord Rector did not recognize Perry's somewhat horrified reactions:

"Among the presents given today, there were 200 bales of rice and each of the 75 wrestlers brought there carried two bales a distance of half a furlong and did tricks with these bales of rice, to the great admiration of Perry, Adams and all the other foreigners. They then went through their practices in wrestling, after which a large number of foreigners did military exercises."

右之外横濱未渡ス々
節相濱ゟ御付
販組士歳入役ニ
吳國人ニ相見セズ

日本力士名前

鏡岩　階ヶ嶽

常山　荒馬

黒岩　象亀

一刀

寶川

黒崎

氷室山

小柳　荒熊

猪王山　雲冕

雲龍　響灘

荒岩　龍峰

高戈山　荒虎

Sumo *wrestlers flip bales of rice while Perry and Adams*
(background) kneel before Japanese lords
(The Mariners Museum, Newport News, Va.)

アメリカ下官ノ族
酔ニ乗ジテ踊遊
ノ圖

河ノ山坂ヨリ。
高ヲさふくんヱ
ルバンシウ。

女子ハふみぶぞ
セ五てるヤ。
バンシウ。

If Perry's admiration was great, it did not show in his later comments on the same day's activities. He called the wrestlers "overfed monsters, whose animal natures had been . . . carefully and successfully developed." As he watched them "glaring with brutal ferocity at each other, ready to exhibit the cruel instincts of a savage nature, it was easy for him to lose all sense of their being human creatures and to persuade himself that he was beholding a couple of brute beasts thirsting for one another's blood."

Negotiations for a treaty went on daily. On March 27 the Americans regaled the Japanese commissioners with a feast and an entertainment on board the flagship *Powhatan,* which flew a Japanese flag to honor the occasion. The Japanese first visited the sloop-of-war *Macedonian.* As they boarded the vessel, a seventeen-gun salute was fired in their honor by the *Mississippi.* From the *Macedonian,* they came to the flag ship, where they were shown through the steamer. They examined the guns and the machinery. A boat was lowered, with a howitzer in its bow, which was repeatedly discharged much to the amusement of the Japanese guests, so the Commodore thought. "Although not a warlike people (at least in their modern history)," the *Narrative* declared in 1856, "the Japanese evidently had a great fondness for martial exercise and display."

There were two banquet tables on board the flagship: one in the Commodore's cabin for the chief dignitaries, the other on the quarter-deck for the rest of the visiting party. Perry noted that the chief Japanese commissioner ate and drank sparingly, but tasted each dish and sipped each different wine. The others proved more solid trenchermen, as did the Japanese party on the deck. The Japanese chief delegate was

Dancing a hornpipe (Black Ship Scroll: Honolulu Academy of Arts)

equally sparing in his comments on the occasion. He wrote in his diary for March 27: "The lord rector and other commissioners went out to the fleet at the eighth hour. They first went to the *Macedonian* and after observing military exercises proceeded to the *Powhatan,* where they dined."

No mention occurs here of what young Spalding called a "capital Ethiopic performance"—an exhibition of minstrelsy got up by sailors, who blacking their faces and dressing themselves in costumes did well enough in Commodore Perry's estimation to "have gained themselves unbounded applause from a New York audience. The gravity of the saturnine Hayashi was not proof against the grotesque exhibition, and even he joined with the rest in the general hilarity provoked by the farcical antics and humorous performances of the mock Negroes."

The next day Perry, Adams and about twenty men came ashore, this time without rifles and pistols.

"Thank you for the hospitality which you extended yesterday to so many of us when we went to your ship," the Lord Rector said.

The Commodore received word that the harbor at Shimoda was satisfactory and consented to its selection as the harbor "in the south." He asked also that the port be opened without delay and added that the two other ports which he considered suitable were Hakodate in the north and Naha in Okinawa. Other matters that came up were the extent to which Americans might walk about in the vicinity of the open harbors.

"Is it not enough that your ships are to be supplied with fuel, water and provision and to be helped when in distress? What profit or benefit can come from allowing your people to walk great distances?" was the question posed in the chief Japanese commissioner's journal.

"Commodore Perry: 'From this time on our ships will come in large numbers. Should our people, upon going ashore, be confined inside narrow limits, it is quite possible that there may be some who will pass beyond the fixed limits, with the result that incidents will arise and cause dissension and confusion. If you now fix wide limits, there will be few who will walk great distances and there will be no trouble from the limits being overstepped; so peace will be preserved forever.

" 'As your nation will become, therefore, a country maintaining friendly relations with our country, none of my countrymen will commit any unlawful act while passing through the villages in the neighborhood of Shimoda. If you reject my proposal, I can only believe that you are not dealing frankly with me; and I shall reject Shimoda and ask that our ships be allowed hereafter to put in somewhere in the vicinity of Yokohama. If you refuse this, I shall be obliged to go to Yedo.' "

The matter was postponed, so Perry raised another question:

" 'What we have arranged is not commerce, but the fact that our ships will hereafter come to Japan makes it necessary for us to send an official to Shimoda. The reason is that when Americans and Japanese enter into disputes, you will have much difficulty settling them, thus causing you much trouble, but if an official be appointed, he will, if you consult him, take matters under his control and arrange them to the advantage and convenience of both sides. In all other foreign countries, an official is sent to each place where there is commerce, and I wish to do the same thing here.' "

The Japanese delegate conceded that such an official had a place where commerce was being conducted, but "where simply fuel, water and provisions are to be supplied, it would seem as though an arrangement of this sort might be dispensed with. Furthermore, no foreigners but Chinese and Hollanders may remain in our country."

The matter was left hanging, the Japanese insisting that his government would never agree and Perry indicating that an envoy would be coming in about eighteen months.

"Let us then discuss this question eighteen months hence," the Lord Rector proposed. These and other matters being generally accepted by both parties, the final version of the treaty could now be prepared.

The treaties were ready for signing. The Japanese were asked to place their seals on the same line with Perry's signature, in accordance with the custom in all countries; but this was refused as contrary to Japanese usage: the seals would be affixed on different sheets.

The next day, March 31, the treaties were exchanged at Yokohama. Three copies signed by Commodore Perry in English with copies in Dutch and Chinese were exchanged for three drafts in Japanese, Chinese and Dutch, signed by the four Japanese commissioners.

"Perry: 'It is a source of great gratification that amity has been established between our two countries.'

"The Lord Rector: 'I am also of this sentiment.'"

It was then agreed that Perry would confer with the Japanese officials in Shimoda, but not until fifty days had elapsed. In the meantime, the American squadron would sail north and examine the port at Hakodate.

After the exchange of treaties Perry presented the Lord Rector with a parcel containing a large American flag, and the other commissioners with maps of the United States. The next day the Japanese were confronted by a puzzling request: the interpreter Antón Portman asked for the brush which the commissioners had used to sign the treaty. He said in his country it would be preserved as a special relic. The reason which finally made some sense to the Japanese was that Perry had signed the treaties before the Japanese's eyes but the Japanese commissioners, following the custom of their country, retired to another room to sign and seal the treaties. "We therefore assume that Portman wished to have the brush as proof, upon their return to their own country, that we had actually signed the treaty," wrote Hayashi.

The treaty having been signed and exchanged, it was sent to Washington with Commander Adams in the *Saratoga*. But Perry still had one ambition which he had not yet realized: to pay an official visit to Edo. He pointed out to the Japanese that it was the custom in all countries for a foreign envoy to be received in audience by the ruler, but, Japanese laws being what they were, he knew that it would be difficult. However, he still wanted to go to Edo, promising not to raise any difficulties, nor do anything unlawful nor create any cause for alarm.

The Japanese delegates were horrified, replying that no foreigners but the Dutch were allowed to enter the capital, that with negotiations over, the commissioners would be embarrassed before their government if Perry went to Edo. Perry understood that the Japanese were in an embarrassing position, but he was in a similar position before his own government. He added then that to avoid giving difficulty to the commissioners he would not go to Edo but that he would steam into Edo Bay and observe the city from his ship. The Japanese still objected.

"If our two countries are to maintain friendly relations, you should do nothing to cause us annoyance: this is essential if we are not to be apprehensive of each other. . . . As our laws must also be obeyed, you should refrain from doing this thing," the Lord Rector wrote that he told Perry.

"Perry: 'If my entering Yedo Bay will cause you such great embarrassment, I shall not do so, but it is possible that I may make a brief turn into it when I leave.'"

Perry spent a day walking around Yokohama, inspecting the countryside and its people. It was during this visit that he saw for the first time the Japanese women's habit of blackening their teeth after marriage. He was entertained in the home of the mayor and met the mayor's wife and sister, who bustled about with a silver sake service.

The American envoy was impressed with the overall appearance of industry and contentment which he saw in all classes of the people, high and low. He saw some signs of poverty, but no evidence of begging. He saw women working in the fields, which he considered evidence of the people's industry. Everywhere he was met with courtesy and curiosity. He concluded that the rigid exclusiveness of Japan was governmental policy, not the sentiments of the people. "Their habits are social among themselves and they frequently intermingle in friendly intercourse," was the way the Commodore's observations were summed up in the *Narrative*. He was particularly impressed by one feature of Japanese society, which he felt proved it superior to all other Asiatic nations, and that was the role of Japanese women, who were recognized as companions, not treated as slaves.

Despite a note from the Japanese delegate remonstrating with him, Perry sent word that on the following day he would approach as near to Edo as the depth of the water in the harbor would permit. April 10 was Commodore Perry's birthday, which gave him perhaps another reason to look for a cause for celebration. The squadron got under way early that morning and moved up the bay. The Japanese interpreters came on board the flagship, appearing greatly concerned at the ships' movement. They begged the Commodore to turn back, plead-

ヘリ買物ノ圖

Commodore Perry (second from left) shopping in Hakodate, May 1854; from a private account with illustration by Matajiro Kojima (Hakodate City Library)

ing that their own lives could be sacrificed in this project. Perry would not be budged, so the interpreters stayed on board to watch the course of the ships. The steamers *Powhatan* and *Mississippi* advanced beyond the other vessels and came so close to forbidden Edo that, but for the fog, the capital would have been distinctly visible. Only the general outlines of the city, however, were discernible. A great number of buildings seemed crowded together over a large area. Around it, on the overlooking heights and promontories, there appeared the usual shapes of canvas forts and fortifications, but they could just as easily have been Buddhist temples hidden by the haze.

One thing was certain to Perry, "that the city of Yedo can be destroyed by a few steamers of very light draught of water and with guns of the heaviest calibre." In addition to his promise not to anchor near the capital, Perry found the tide too strong for safe steerage and so decided to turn about. The Commodore knew the fears of the Japanese commissioners, whose lives would be endangered by any closer approach to Edo, so he yielded:

"He thought it was better not to bring about an issue that might endanger the very friendly position in which he had placed himself in relation to the Japanese. It would have been a source of endless regret, too, if to gratify a profitless curiosity misfortune should have been brought upon the commissioners, whose friendly conduct deserved every kind of return that might be given in consonance with duty. The squadron, therefore now returned and anchored at the American Anchorage. The anxiety of the Japanese interpreters, who remained on board, during the whole trip, was thus much relieved."

One of the interpreters was aboard the *Mississippi* during this foray into the inner waters of Edo Bay. Young Spalding was made to understand that if the ships anchored off Edo, it would at once require the interpreters to commit suicide—to save themselves and their families from dishonor.

Hayashi, the chief Japanese commissioner, described the day:

"All the seven American warships being about to leave, the censor Hirayama Kenjiro, the police officer Aihara Isaburo, the interpreter Moriyama Einosuke, and others went out to Perry's ships to bid him farewell. As Perry had said that he would, when leaving, make a brief turn into Yedo Bay, they brought word from Mimasaka-no-kami and Udono that everyone was apprehensive and that they earnestly desired him not to enter Yedo Bay. Perry told Kenjiro that he was about to sail and would make a turn into Yedo Bay, and that the officials should remain on board and see for themselves that he would do nothing unlawful. Kenjiro tried in various ways to deter Perry, but he would not listen. Everyone was greatly concerned. Then two of the steamers gradually steamed towards Yedo. No salutes were fired at Kanagawa, and it was feared that, should the warships fire salutes when they entered Yedo Bay, great alarm would be created in the Capital. Einosuke was determined, if he saw signs of a salute about to be fired, he would place himself before the cannon's mouth and so sacrifice his life. The two steamers stopped when the Haneda Light was visible in the distance. Perry summoned Einosuke and asked if the place where a lighthouse could be seen were Yedo. Einosuke replied that it was and that Japanese sailing ships whose masts could be seen ahead were already in Yedo Bay; whereupon Perry called some of his officers and drawing out a telescope looked through it. 'How clearly,' he said, 'Yedo can be seen!' When his officers had also looked through the telescope, he said, 'Having now seen Yedo, let us go,' and he had the ship turned towards the south. He then said to Einosuke that the officials could now leave. How great had been their anxiety! But he had been ordered by his government and he had no choice. If it had been entirely left to his discretion, he would have done nothing to cause the commissioners any embarrassment, but he was accompanied by many men, and as there were some who did not agree with him he had no choice but to do what he did. However, having shown Yedo to all, no one could say upon their return that they had not seen Yedo; and he was therefore without any concern. He was grateful to all of us and asked that his regards be conveyed to the Lord Rector and the other commissioners. He was very polite when making his farewells."

Since there was no reason to stay any longer in the upper bay of Edo, Commodore Perry prepared to leave. On April 18, the *Powhatan,* accompanied by the *Mississippi,* headed for Shimoda, where the *Vandalia, Southampton, Supply* and *Lexington* were already anchored.

With negotiations over, each delegation evaluated the treaty and its own success or failure.

The Japanese report to the Bakufu, signed by the four commissioners, read:

"The American envoy Perry, having last year presented to the Bakufu a letter from his country's President and believing that since the Bakufu accepted delivery of this letter it would grant the requests made therein, recently requested the Bakufu to give him a written reply expressing its consent. Were the Bakufu not to agree, he said, he would have failed to accomplish his mission; and even at the cost of unavoidable war he could not return to his own country without succeeding in these requests. He had accordingly arranged to bring several warships with him, and still more were being sent from his home country. This being so, the Bakufu ordered us to undertake discussions and negotiations on this matter, giving us secret instructions, however, that we were to handle the matter peaceably. In accordance with these instructions we have conducted negotiations and concluded a treaty.

"When the negotiations began, the foreigners brought with

them a draft of the treaty they sought and urged that we conform fully to their wishes [as expressed in it]. In the course of the discussions we succeeded in modifying this and reducing it to what is shown in the enclosure.

"We informed Perry that the Bakufu had last year asked the Dutch Kapitan [at Deshima] to inform him that the question of a written reply must be postponed, since a new reign was starting and the great pressure of business in domestic affairs made an immediate answer impossible; but that since he had come none the less, officials had been sent to conduct negotiations and he would receive a reply from the persons so sent after discussions had been held. Thus the matter was settled without giving him any written reply from the Bakufu. Moreover, the agreement was concluded in the names of the four envoys, without any official document from the Rōjū.

"Perry stated repeatedly that when American castaways landed in Japan the Bakufu had hitherto treated them as enemies, immediately imprisoning them in confined quarters. This was to treat them like criminals, he said, and was assuredly an inhuman policy. In his country human life was highly valued. It was therefore his desire that the Bakufu should in the future treat castaways in the same way as they were treated in other countries, no distinction being made between foreigners and ourselves. We accordingly informed him that human life was, of course, highly valued in our country too, and that castaways not only of his country but also of all other countries invariably received kind treatment. However, we said, when these castaways without our consent took matters into their own hands it was not possible to treat them in this way. We would not hereafter treat them as prisoners if they were peaceable, but we would certainly have to punish any who broke our country's laws.

"With respect to the request that we provide food, wood,

water, and other supplies needed by ships, we informed them that we would agree to this because such things were vital to human life. We would, moreover, provide coal, which with the development of navigation in recent years has become an article of daily use in his country; but since this was an article not much used in Japan, we said, it could be supplied only to the extent that it was available at any specific place. We also stated it as the Bakufu's intention to provide such things as food, wood, water, and coal free of charge for a period of three to five years, but Perry said that they never accepted goods from other countries without payment and that he must therefore request that they be allowed to offer something in return. We replied that they were quite free to offer something by way of acknowledgement.

"The foreigners stated that our work would really be incomplete unless we decided upon the ports at which the Bakufu was to provide food, wood, water, and so on. They asked that we should open Ryūkyū [Loochoo], Hakodate, and three other ports, and also that one of these ports should be Uraga. We informed them that Ryūkyū was a distant frontier outpost about which we could give no answer; nor could a decision be taken at once about Hakodate, because it was in the territory of one of the feudal lords. Still less could permission be granted for Uraga, we told them, as it was a place much frequented by Japanese vessels. Perry then asked that Kanagawa-Yokohama be made one of the ports and suggested various places that he would like opened. We accordingly had no choice [in the end] but to open Shimoda in Izu and Hakodate in Matsumae and designate them as places at which food, wood, water, and so on would be provided.

"We proposed an agreement by which the Bakufu would provide food, wood, water, coal, and so on at Nagasaki, but the foreigners stated that Nagasaki was not suitable for their

世町ニ高魚ヲ
ヒ喜悦シテ
中ニ帰ルノ図

北亜黒利加花政治州之使節
ペリ之真像

Sailors with fresh fish bought in Shimoda (Black Ship Scroll: Honolulu Academy of Arts)

country and they probably would not go there at first. They asked that these facilities be provided at the two ports of Shimoda and Hakodate. However, they said, only fishing-vessels would go in numbers to Hakodate, so coal would not be needed there. At that place only food, wood, water, and other supplies necessary to ships would be required.

"The foreigners urged that if food, wood, water, and so on were to be supplied at Shimoda, then they would want to be able to move about freely in the vicinity of Shimoda harbour. We replied that it was our intention to prescribe bounds in the immediate vicinity of the harbour within which they could move about. However, they insisted that they must be free to act as they chose in this, without being restricted in any way, and claimed that they wished first to make a chart of Shimoda harbour and then to be allowed to walk for pleasure within a distance of one day's travel [from that place], which is a distance of seven *ri*. . . . We advanced various arguments to show that this was impossible, saying that it was in any case our intention to set wide bounds within which they could move about, but they were most insistent that if we did so they would [consider themselves free to] land at will elsewhere on the coast and even go to Edo itself. They would by no means accept our suggestion; and we realized on careful consideration that if we left the matter like this they would certainly land hereafter at a number of [other] places and that this trivial detail might well lead to the outbreak of hostilities. To grant this foreign request would assuredly be no light matter; yet if we proved stubborn in discussing it they might, after all, land and walk about wherever they chose, not only at Shimoda but at a number of other places as well, and we would be helpless [to prevent it]. Hence rather than leave the foreigners to land and act violently [elsewhere] and so provoke hostilities, we decided it would be better to allow them to move about in the vincinity of the one port of Shimoda. However, we reached agreement with them that having once decided on the two ports of Shimoda and Hakodate, no ships would ever enter any other port, except for the special case of vessels in distress.

"They also requested similar arrangements for walking at Hakodate, but we told them that a reply to this would be made after further investigation, since Hakodate was not only distant but was also part of the territories of one of the feudal lords.

"The envoy Perry frequently expressed a desire to go to Edo, but by citing our national laws as the reason we eventually succeeded in making him accept our refusal of this. Then he said he wanted to survey Edo Bay, urging that the sea was common to all countries and could not be divided into 'ours' and 'theirs'; moreover, he said, he had no evil purpose, his sole object being to make a survey. However, we insisted on refusing this, on the grounds that to let him enter Edo Bay would cause disturbance in the capital, while our nationals laws forbade the entrance of foreign ships into Edo Bay. When we pointed out that having granted most of his requests we must really insist on his observing our national laws in this one matter, he was forced to agree.

"With regard to the question of trade, Perry presented a paper drawn up in accordance with the regulations governing trade between his country and China and proposed that we begin negotiations on that basis. We refused this, however, pointing out that in Japan we had little experience of trade and could not lightly permit it; that the main theme of his present request was kind treatment for the citizens of his country and we had, after full consideration, given an undertaking to provide wood, water, and so on; that trade was conducted entirely with a view to profit on both sides, having no relevance to considerations of humanity, and that we were therefore unable to discuss this question at the present time. There was accordingly no further discussion of this matter in the subsequent negotiations.

"He asked us to open Shimoda harbour at once, so we informed him that it would be impossible to do so until the third month of next year [17 April–15 May 1855]. He then said that if the text of the treaty did not state that at least one port would be opened at once, the United States President would certainly consider that he had failed in his mission; and, moreover, that this would only be a paper provision, for he was sure no ships would actually go there before the third month of next year, though since wood and water would be wanted at all places where ships might go, it might happen that ships would ask for wood and water there before that time. We said we would agree only on this understanding and asked him to state his acceptance thereof in writing. And though he was reluctant to send us such a letter, he was eventually persuaded to do so.

"In these negotiations with the foreigners, our country sent no written reply to their letter and the business was concluded by us whom you sent for that purpose, without any official letter from the Rōjū. By this, our national prestige was maintained.

"The envoy Perry was persuaded to abandon his idea of going to Edo and of circumnavigating Edo Bay and surveying there. By this, respect for our national laws was preserved.

"As evidence that he would have no future designs on Japan, the envoy presented a flag to [Hayashi] Daigaku-no-kami and cannon to [Ido] Tsushima-no-kami and [Izawa] Mimasaka-no-kami. He said that should Japan hereafter suffer foreign attack we could use these in repelling it and that the United States would come to our aid with similar weapons. By this, our national prestige was maintained.

"It is the custom of all countries that when a treaty is con-

下田ノ大安寺ニ
オイラ遊女ノ
姿ヲウツシ
アメリカ國王へ
一覧ニ備ヘント
心ヲ配ル
圖

文唐通詞シツトム

Left, sailor with Japanese women; above, a photographic sitting
(Black Ship Scroll: Honolulu Academy of Arts)

cluded the representatives of both countries meet and affix their seals in each other's presence. Thinking greater respect due our country, we refused to seal the treaty jointly [with Perry] and arranged that each party should use a separate copy of the text, ourselves employing one to which we had previously affixed our seals. He said that if this was the custom of our country he must necessarily conform to it, but added in a letter he sent us on the following day that when he returned home this might be thought improper in an envoy. By this, our national prestige was maintained.

"We regret to report that after texts of the treaty had been exchanged he sent us a letter stating that while he accepted the admonitions we had issued on the basis of our national laws, it might not be possible in the future for those laws to continue indefinitely in their present form.

"The text of the treaty was agreed as in the enclosure herewith, but there were also a number of other matters which he wished to add. Had we discussed them at this time, we believe he would have turned to the questions of the immediate establishment of consulates and the dispatch of officials to Japan. But when the time comes that we have to accept the dispatch of officials to Japan, the treaty will have to be further expanded.

"It was our object in these negotiations to win him away from any previous idea he had of opening hostilities and to temper our admonitions with leniency, thus completing the whole affair in peace: and at the same time we sought to handle the discussions in such a way as to bring no disgrace upon our country.

"Submitted with respect."

The news of Perry's achievement did not reach the American public until June 13, 1854. That day the *New York*

Times printed a somewhat inaccurate report of the treaty, but it glowed with pride for the American accomplishment. Its feature headline, only one column in width, read: "JAPAN OPENED.—Satisfactory Result of Commodore Perry's Visit.— Three Ports Opened to American Trade [sic]—Agreement to Furnish Coal to American Steamers—" etc.

"The *Susquehanna* arrived at Hong Kong from Japan on the 2d [April] bringing the gratifying intelligence that Commodore Perry had succeeded in the objects of his mission in a manner that will confer honor on his country and enduring fame on himself. The precise terms of a Commercial Treaty had not been definitively arranged when the *Susquehanna* left the Yedo on the 24th of March; but enough had been done to establish a friendly feeling between the two countries. *The opening of Three or more ports to the Commerce of America [sic], and the furnishing of Coals for its Steamers, may be considered as matters settled,* and Captain Adams held himself in readiness to proceed in the *Saratoga* to bear the intelligence to the Government at Washington.

"We are enabled to furnish our readers with a detailed narrative of the proceedings in Japan, from which it will be seen that nothing could have been better or more fortunate than the course pursued by Commodore Perry. Indeed we feel pretty certain that the most skillful diplomatist in Europe could not have brought matters to so speedy, pacific and successful an issue. Commodore Perry was known as a brave as well as accomplished seaman, but it was thought he had rather a propensity for fighting, which indeed with such means at his disposal, and such peoples to deal with as the Japanese were ignorantly presumed to be, was deemed inevitable by most people though, as our pages show, not by every one. Here however he has disappointed the world, and perhaps not a few in his squadron; but he has done what we did not do in China and it was not expected any one could accomplish in Japan—*he has peacefully and amiably opened it to the intercourse of his countrymen, without firing a shot or using an angry word.*"

In his personal journal, the Commodore recorded his satisfaction at the successful conclusion of his mission:

"The great object of effecting an advantageous compact with this singular people has been fully accomplished. This compact secures protection and kind treatment to all Americans who may by chance or design find themselves in any part of the empire. It also stipulates to give shelter and supplies to vessels of the United States, and to grant to American citizens privileges never conceded to any foreign people in the two preceding centuries. The government of the United States may well claim the honor of being the first to open friendly and *independent* relations with a nation hitherto claiming the right of entire exclusion from all foreign intercourse, unless the immunities granted to the Dutch and Chinese at Nagasaki, may be considered in such light."

The *Narrative of the Expedition* gives the official estimate:

"The whole treaty shows that the purpose of the Japanese was to try the experiment of intercourse with us before they made it as extensive or as intimate as it is between us and the Chinese. It was all they would do at the time, and much, very much, was obtained on the part of our negotiator in procuring a concession even to this extent.

"But, as he knew that our success would be but the forerunner of that of other powers, as he believed that new relations of trade once commenced, not only with ourselves but with England, France, Holland, and Russia, in the progress of events, could not fail effectually and forever not only to break up the old restrictive policy and open Japan to the world, but must also lead gradually to liberal commercial treaties, he wisely, in the ninth article, without 'consultation or delay,' secured to the United States and their citizens all privileges and advantages which Japan might hereafter 'grant to any other nation or nations.'

"As far as we have yet learned, all other powers have been content to obtain just what we, as pioneers, have obtained. Their treaties are like ours. That of Russia is copied from ours, with no change but that of the substitution of the port of Nagasaki for Napha in Lew Chew. We respectfully submit, that all, and indeed more than all, under the circumstances, that could reasonably have been expected, has been accomplished. Japan has been opened to the nations of the west. It is not to be believed, that having once effected an entrance, the enlightened powers that have made treaties with her will *go backward,* and, by any indiscretion, lose what, after so many unavailing efforts for centuries, has at last been happily attained. It belongs to these nations to show Japan that her interests will be promoted by communication with them. As prejudice gradually vanishes, we may hope to see the future negotiation of more and more liberal commercial treaties, for the benefit not of ourselves only, but of all the maritime powers of Europe, for the advancement of Japan, and for the upward progress of our common humanity. It would be a foul reproach to Christendom now to force Japan to relapse into her cheerless and unprogressive state of unnatural isolation. She is the youngest sister in the circle of commercial nations. Let those who are older kindly take her by the hand, and aid her tottering steps, until she has reached a vigor that will enable her to walk firmly in her own strength. Cautious and kindly treatment now will soon lead to commercial treaties as liberal as can be desired."

4. TOWNSEND HARRIS:

THE TREATY OF AMITY AND COMMERCE

Artist's conception of an American train moving, 1861; print by Utagawa Yoshikazu (Courtesy, Museum of Fine Arts, Boston)

While Commodore Perry was in Shanghai in 1853, making final preparations for his squadron's initial visit to Japan, Townsend Harris, an American businessman in China, was exerting every effort to have himself included in the expedition. His attempt, however, was not successful. Harris was an educator-turned-merchant, who had become interested in the diplomatic relations between the United States and the Far East. Failing with Perry, he sought instead the post of American consul at Hong Kong or at Canton, but he managed only to get an appointment to a minor consulate at Ningpo (an important port in northeast China), which had no appeal for him. Then the news came that Perry had concluded the Convention of 1854, which provided for an American consular representative in Japan. Harris at once set himself to winning the new, exciting and responsible assignment—America's first consul to Japan.

Townsend Harris had unusual qualifications for the post. He had been president of the Board of Education in New York and one of the guiding spirits in founding the City College of New York. In 1848 he resigned, and for the next six years traveled around Asia and the Pacific in his own merchant vessel, visiting many islands in the South Seas, touching the Chinese mainland, New Zealand and the Philippines. He crossed the China Sea to trade both with North and South China. He had both traded and lived in Shanghai, Ningpo, Canton, Macao, Singapore, Ceylon and India. In a few years he had obtained experience which few could match. He had learned to live with many different peoples, to do business with them and to view their manners and customs with tolerance, sympathy and, above all, patience.

Harris hurried back to the United States to make his bid for the consular post in Japan. After a voyage of eight weeks he reached New York just one month after the Perry treaty had been proclaimed. It had been ratified and signed by President Franklin Pierce the year before. In February 1855 an exchange of ratification had taken place in Shimoda, Japan. Among Harris' supporters was Commodore Perry, and on August 4, 1855, he was named United States Consul General for Japan. On the same day, before word of his appointment reached him, Harris wrote to President Pierce with almost prophetic insight into what the future held for him:

"I have a perfect knowledge of the social banishment I must endure while in Japan, and the mental isolation in which I must live, and am prepared to meet it. I am a single man, without ties to cause me to look anxiously to my old home, or to become impatient in my new one."

On his way to Japan Harris was instructed to stop off in Siam and arrange for a commercial treaty with that kingdom. The Navy steam frigate, *San Jacinto,* Commodore James Armstrong commanding, was ordered to meet Harris at Penang and take him to Bangkok, Siam, and then to Shimoda, Japan.

Harris journeyed to his post through London and Paris, where he bought "some properly ornamental clothes" to wear at the royal court of Siam and "a good supply of shoes." He conferred with American consuls in France and proceeded to Marseilles, Malta, Egypt and then Calcutta and Penang, where he arrived in January 1856. The *San Jacinto* did not reach its rendezvous with Harris until two months later, after an unhurried passage from New York of 149 days. Harris was warmly welcomed aboard and saluted with thirteen guns as he returned to shore. By mid-April 1856 the treaty with Siam was concluded in Bangkok and Harris moved on to Hong Kong, where he waited impatiently while the *San Jacinto* went into dry dock to have her propellers repaired. In August the steamer was ready and Harris was on the last lap of his journey to Japan.

Off the coast of Japan, the ship ran along the edge of a typhoon and rolled wildly. Harris was thrown out of his chair and his left hip and leg bruised. It was almost impossible to write while the ship plowed through the heavy seas, but Harris faithfully kept his daily journal. He was beset by conflicting emotions. His sense of history was strong, and he felt the role he might possibly be called on to play. In his journal for Monday, August 18, 1856, he wrote:

"Mental and social isolation on the one hand, and on the other are important public duties which, if properly discharged, will redound to my credit. A people almost unknown to the world is to be examined and reported on in its social, moral and political state; and productions of the country—animal, vegetable and mineral—to be ascertained; the products of the industry of the country found out, and its capacity for commercial intercourse, what are its wants, and what it has to give in exchange. A new and difficult language to be learned; a history, which may throw some light on that of China and Korea, to be examined; and finally, the various religious creeds of Japan are to be looked at. These various matters offer abundant occupation for my mind, and will prevent anything like ennui being felt if I only give myself heartily to the work and if that *sine qua non* of all earthly occupation —health—be vouchsafed to me by the Great Giver of all good."

That night Townsend Harris' mind was too filled with the excitement of his new duties in Japan to let him sleep. He tried every way he knew to calm his nerves, including the well-known air bath proposed by Benjamin Franklin. But nothing worked; he tossed restlessly until four in the morning.

The following day turned out bright and beautiful, with a fair wind. An albatross flew by, the first he had seen in six years. Seventy miles to the west lay Japan's southern island of Kyushu, but an empty sea stretched to the horizon; not a sail, ship nor boat of any kind was to be seen. Harris could not keep the thoughts of his mission from crowding his mind.

"I shall be the first recognized agent from a civilized power to reside in Japan," he noted. "This forms an epoch in my life and may be the beginning of a new order of things in Japan. I hope I may so conduct myself that I may have honorable mention in the histories which will be written on Japan and its future destiny."

Shimoda was still 344 miles away.

The next day's run brought the Americans 180 miles closer. Some Japanese ships appeared, but they showed signs of anxiety and alarm and would not stop or speak to the foreign steamer. Finally, on August 21, Harris had his first glimpse of Japanese soil: Cape Omaye, overlooking a stretch of sea filled with some seventy fishing boats.

"[I] like the appearance of the Japanese, clean and well-clad, cheerful looking, pretty fish-boats," he confided to his journal.

Harris was accompanied by a secretary, Henry C. J. Heusken, who acted also as his Dutch translator. A boat, flying both the American Stars and Stripes and the black and white striped flag of Japan, brought out a pilot, who steered the big ship into the harbor of Shimoda. Harris looked around at the port which Perry had opened up and concluded that the inner harbor was too small to hold more than three vessels as big as the San Jacinto at one time. The outer harbor appeared to him as not much more than a roadstead. It was more a bight than a harbor, not really suited for shipping. Moreover, it was separated from Edo by mountainous country, which the Japanese

Shimoda, sketch by Henry C. J. Heusken (New York Public Library)

probably hoped would keep foreigners away from the capital.

Arrangements were quickly made for the new American consular agent to come ashore and be received by the Magistrate of Shimoda. The meeting originally was set for the day after Harris' arrival, but it soon became apparent that the Japanese would be happy to delay it. The reasons were not hidden long. Commodore Armstrong of the *San Jacinto* had been taken suddenly ill and would not have been able to accompany Harris for the Friday reception. The Japanese officials, on the other hand, did not know quite how to handle this American consul and hoped that, by combining his visit with the Commodore's, they would blur the distinctiveness of each. The Magistrate of Shimoda suddenly pleaded illness, but Harris insisted that he would land and pay his official call regardless of any excuses or illnesses.

Harris meanwhile visited the small fishing village, Kaki-zaki, opposite Shimoda, where a Shinto shrine had been set aside to accommodate the Americans. The shrine was roomy, neat and very clean. It would do quite well for a stay of a few weeks, Harris observed.

Harris' official call on the Magistrate of Shimoda took place on the morning of Monday, August 25. Three boatloads of American sailors preceded him as an escort from the *San Jacinto,* which fired a thirteen-gun salute as he pulled away. He was conducted through streets thronged with curious Japanese to a new building in the center of town. Shimoda had been rebuilt since an earthquake and tidal wave had destroyed it in December 1854. The official received the American consul politely and inquired in whose honor the ship had fired the salute. When he learned that the salute was in Harris' honor, the American consul immediately seemed to rise in his estimation.

That day marked the beginnings of real negotiations between Harris and the Japanese.

"Our visit lasted nearly two hours, and we were all much pleased with the appearance and manners of the Japanese," Harris wrote in his journal for August 25, 1856. "I repeat, they are superior to any people east of the Cape of Good Hope."

The Saturday before, Harris and his secretary had gone ashore to inspect a temple in Shimoda which had also been assigned as a residence for Americans. Harris was less pleased with this building than with the one in the fishing village across the bay. The temple in Shimoda was not in the open; it was enclosed by a hill which shut off the air and the prevailing winds; it was surrounded by stagnant pools and what he called "other disagreeables." Nevertheless, at first he was determined that he would abide by the letter of the treaty, as well as his instructions from the United States government, which ordered him to take up residence in Shimoda.

The day after his meeting with the Magistrate of Shimoda saw the beginning of Harris' real difficulties with the Japanese. He was informed bluntly that Japan had not been expecting a consul from America; that a consul was to be sent only if some difficulty arose between the two countries and no such problem had come up; that Shimoda had not yet recovered from the earthquake and tidal wave of 1854 and no suitable residence for a foreign diplomat was ready; and that he should go away and come back in about a year.

The Japanese interpreted the Perry treaty to read that a consul would come to Japan if both countries desired it, not if the United States alone wished to send one. For several hours these arguments, in one form or another, were politely presented to the American consul, who just as courteously "firmly negatived all their propositions."

That same day Harris ordered some tall spars to make a flagpole from which to fly the American flag.

Japanese objections to Harris' arrival were not set aside so easily. The day following Harris arrived for a meeting with the officials of Shimoda only to find they had broken the appointment without even notifying him. In their place was a functionary from Edo, who claimed that he outranked the Shimoda magistrate. But Harris was not prepared to accept the verbal claims of the new arrival and threatened to make plans with Commodore Armstrong to steam straight up to Edo to finish his business in the capital itself. Harris knew from Perry's experience that the mere mention of approaching Edo would create agitation among the Japanese officials. Harris was firm, insisting that a place of residence be assigned to him

at once and that the Magistrate of Shimoda apologize for breaking his appointment.

The tidy temple in the fishing village was offered to him
with many explanations that the village was really included
in the port of Shimoda and that it was only a temporary solu-
tion until an appropriate building could be erected. It was the
best they had to offer, the Japanese insisted, pointing out that
they could not be accused of refusing to receive the American
dignitary or to furnish him with proper quarters. After some
hesitation, Harris accepted the residence at Kakizaki even
though he stated that he might be blamed by his government
for not insisting on Shimoda. It was understood that a suitable
house would be prepared for him as soon as possible.

The spars that Harris had ordered for his flagpole were delivered, but they were not as tall as he had wanted. Poles fifty
feet high could only be obtained in the mountains, he was
told. The Consul carefully jotted down the comparative costs
and then chose the shorter, cheaper masts, thinking he had
saved seventy-five dollars. A day or so later he found out that
the pole for his flagstaff would cost seventy-eight dollars—"an
enormous price!" he exclaimed in his notebook.

On September 1, the Magistrate of Shimoda was replaced
by his alternate from Edo. The new official appeared to
Harris dark and sullen. The American wrote that he regretted
the change and feared trouble with the new official, with
whom he would have to deal for the next six months. Harris'
estimate turned out quite incorrect. The new magistrate was
Inouye, Shinano-no-kami, who was to become one of the
American's best friends in Japan.

But the new official renewed the arguments against acceptance of a foreign consul and Harris rejected them all once
more. What was the secret reason for the United States' hav-

ing sent an agent? Harris was asked. He answered straightfor-
wardly that he knew of none except the rights granted in the
Perry treaty. Would Harris write to the American government
and ask that he be recalled? No, he would not. Did the Commodore of the *San Jacinto* have the authority to take him
away? No, the Commodore was a naval officer under orders,
who had done his duty by delivering the American diplomat to
Japan. Would the Commodore carry a letter back to the
United States government? No, any communication from the
Japanese government would have to go through diplomatic
channels. Harris assured the Japanese officials that he would
make a full report on everything that had happened, but that
no reply could be expected unless an official letter from the
Japanese Minister for Foreign Affairs was sent. Such a letter
would get an immediate answer.

The discussion was about old trivialities, covering old
ground, as far as Harris was concerned. It consumed many
useless hours, but that day Harris' baggage and supplies were
landed in good order. As Harris took leave of the Navy
steamer, the crew climbed the rigging to send him off with
three cheers and the band struck up "Hail Columbia." In this
fashion the day was marked when the first American consul
went ashore to take up residence on the soil of Japan. Harris
was welcomed to his new home by the Vice-Magistrate of Shimoda and a suite of other officials, who brought him presents
of fowl, eggs and lobsters. The following morning the flagpole
was erected before the Consul's quarters and in the early afternoon, with some of the ship's company forming a circle round
the tall spar, Harris hoisted the first consular flag ever to fly in
Japan.

"Grim reflections," he wrote in his journal that day. "Ominous change—undoubted beginning of the end. Query—if for
the real good of Japan?"

That night the American man-of-war steamed out of the harbor, dipping its flag in salute to the solitary American diplomat. That night, also, his first in his official residence in Japan, Harris slept well.

The Japanese were accustomed to setting observers (or spies) to watch over the activities of foreigners, and they sought to reserve several rooms in Harris' quarters supposedly for officials to "guard" him. Harris let it be known quite definitely that he would have no one in his house who was not of his own choosing; he would tolerate no government watchers or guards of any kind on or near his premises. The Japanese reluctantly agreed.

Slowly the American began to receive friendlier visits. The interpreter, Enosuke Moriyama, who had been so active in the negotiations with Commodore Perry, paid a call of friendship, as the Japanese called it. But what Harris called "flare-ups" still continued with the officialdom in Shimoda. On Septem-

Townsend Harris' house at Shimoda,
by Henry C. J. Heusken (New York Public Library)

ber 11 he wrote in exasperation that the Japanese functionaries "told me some egregious lies in answer to some requests I made." "I told them plainly that I knew they lied; that, if they wished me to have any confidence in them, they must always speak the truth; that if I asked anything they were not authorized to grant, or about which they wished to consult, let them simply say they were not prepared to answer me, but that to tell lies to me was treating me like a child, and that I should consider myself insulted thereby; that in my country a man who lied was disgraced, and that to call a man a liar was the greatest insult that could be given; that I hoped they would, for the future, if they told me anything, simply tell me the truth, and then I should respect them, which I could not do when they told me falsehoods."

For the next two months Harris spent his time walking around the countryside, making notes of the vegetation and flowers, observing where improvements could be made, enduring some discomforts and annoyances from servants, houseboys and greedy shopkeepers. He suffered a few minor injuries and had several bouts with his constant ill health. His Japanese visitors kept him busy explaining Western customs and laws. In return he asked about Japanese manners and traditions. He noted how much bloodier some Japanese laws were than similar American regulations: for example, Japan exacted the death penalty not only for murder but also for arson, burglary and "for violent deportment toward a father." On the other hand the Japanese found it difficult to understand that imprisonment could be much of a punishment, since it provided the law-breaker with good shelter, plenty of food and clothing—which could not be much of a hardship to many men. "As they never walk for pleasure they [the imprisoned criminals] cannot think it hard to be deprived of wandering about," seemed to express the Japanese attitude.

Harris discovered that owning a horse would increase his importance in Japanese eyes, so he paid twenty-six dollars for a mount. He also ordered a *norimono*. Harris bathed in cold water, which astonished his Japanese friends, who preferred the boiling hot mineral springs in which the country abounded. Japanese bathing habits shocked the American, who noted in his diary that the Japanese were "a *clean* people." "Everyone bathes every day. There are many public bath houses. The wealthy people have their baths in their own houses, but the working classes all, of both sexes, old and young, enter the same bathroom and there perform ablutions in a state of perfect nudity. I cannot account for so indelicate a proceeding on the part of a people so generally correct."

On October 4 Harris celebrated his fifty-second birthday with: "God grant that the short remainder of my life may be more usefully and honorably spent than the preceding and larger portion of it." The day before a Dutch steamer had departed after a two-day visit in Shimoda. From the ship's captain Harris had learned that the Japanese were having two steamships built in Holland. The day after Harris' birthday, the American schooner *General Pierce* arrived from the northern Japanese port of Hakodate, which was to be officially opened to American ships the following year. The schooner left carrying Harris' first dispatches to Washington.

On October 25 Harris sent word to the head of the Japanese Council of State in Edo that he had a letter from President Franklin Pierce of the United States for the Emperor of Japan, which he wanted to deliver in person. In his letter to Edo Harris included a tantalizing offer to reveal some secrets of importance to the Japanese government about the intentions of the British toward Japan. The difference between the

Emperor and the Shogun had not yet been made clear to the American.

Five days later, October 30, became in Harris' journal an important day in the history of Japan. For the first time the magistrate of a Japanese city was to break an ancient law and pay a visit to a foreigner's residence. Both officials of Shimoda, together with their assistants, arrived at Harris' home, where they were entertained lavishly for most of the afternoon. Harris found the Japanese honorary title "no-kami" puzzling.

"The Governors are of the highest rank of any men in Japan after the vassal Princes, being *no-Kami*—i.e. men so learned that nothing can be taught them, and so sublimated in goodness that they rank in name—*Kami*—with the demi-gods of Japan," Harris noted, adding, however: "This word—*Kami* —has a variety of meanings—e.g. demi-god, noble, paper and hair."

During their four-hour visit Harris began instructing the Japanese officials in the ways of the West, beginning with an account of the coastal survey activities of the maritime nations.

But for the next two months the American consul was still confined to Shimoda, taking long walks, visiting the hot sulphur springs, welcoming visiting vessels, meeting their captains, writing dispatches and trying to keep well and warm. He noted wryly in his journal for November 4: "I have a smoky house, but luckily no scolding wife."

On Christmas Day 1856 the solitary bachelor could feel keenly the loneliness of his situation. For the previous eight years he had spent Christmas Day either at sea, or in such ports as Manila, Pula Penang, Singapore, Hong Kong, Calcutta and Ceylon. "Merry Christmas," he wrote to himself.

"How happy are those who live in lands where these joyous greetings can be exchanged! As for me, I am sick and solitary, living as one may say in a prison—a large one it is true—but still a prison." As the year ended he could only recall how many events of importance had happened to him during the year, yet he was low spirited—both from ill health and from the slowness of the progress he was making with the Japanese. On New Year's Day he passed the hours imagining himself making calls on friends in New York. In Japan no one came to call or exchange greetings.

The new year did not quicken the pace of Harris' dealings with the Japanese. Word came back that an answer had been received to Harris' letter to Edo, written almost three months before. Was the answer in writing? Harris asked. No, he was answered, it was not, since Japanese law forbade the writing of letters to foreigners. Harris told the governors that such a statement was ridiculous since he knew that letters had been written to Commodore Perry, to the Russians and to the Dutch. He told the Japanese officials, "To assert such palpable falsehoods was to treat me like a child and that, if they repeated it, I should feel myself insulted."

He spent January studying the flowers, learning the first rudiments of the Japanese language and trying to keep up his health, which was generally poor. He had lost forty pounds in the year past, and still he recorded in mid-January: "Ill, ill, ill. I have cured the 'Saint Anthony's Fire,' but I am constantly wasting away in flesh."

For the first six months of his residence in Japan Harris was not invited inside the home of any Japanese in Shimoda, much to his disappointment. It was not until late February 1857 that he received an invitation from the Magistrate of Shimoda to visit him and the co-magistrate in their private residence. The event was another break in Japan's long-established way of treating foreigners.

Washington's Birthday, February 22, fell on a Sunday that year, and Harris obtained Japanese agreement to hold off the official celebration until the next day, when two brass howitzers were loaned him to fire the official salutes. The Japanese rather proudly let the American know that they had a thousand cannon made from the one that Commodore Perry had given them as a present in 1854. Harris was not inclined to believe their boast.

Harris had to exercise all his patience waiting for an official answer to his letter to Edo. Consultation on matters of smaller importance was speeded up as the Shimoda officials became empowered to deal with them on the spot, but larger questions still had to be referred to the Bakufu. Early in March an American bark arrived with year-old newspapers and the news that the president of the United States was now James Buchanan. Harris, alone in a strange land, out of touch with his own government, straining to get on with his mission to negotiate a treaty of commerce with Japan, found himself sicker than he had been for years as the spring of 1857 drew near. The ailing American consul was vomiting blood. All around him the weather was turning fine. He looked out to see the wheat growing, potatoes being planted, and the lovely Japanese camelia tree, twenty feet tall, in his front yard, bursting into a thousand blossoms. Early in April he began to plant his own garden. The peach and cherry trees began to bloom.

Harris' letter to the Japanese minister in Edo, however, had not been forgotten. The officials in Shimoda tried every ingenious device to get him to disclose the special information

Townsend Harris, by James Bogle (Courtesy of the City College of New York)

which he had hinted at. At the same time Harris kept pressing for all his rights as a diplomat, and he was not above using threats to back up his demands. He wanted the right to make his purchases and to pay for them directly without the interference of any government agent. He wanted the fact accepted that as a consul he could travel anywhere in the whole Empire of Japan, and he let it be understood that he daily expected an American man-of-war to come to Shimoda. The warship's mission was to pick up diplomatic dispatches, but its cannon could reinforce Harris' requests, he hinted.

Inouye, the Magistrate of Shimoda, continued his visits to Harris, as did the interpreter Moriyama. Both the magistrate and the interpreter were growing friendlier with the American diplomat. Moriyama explained the workings of the Shogunate to Harris, revealing that the Ziogoon, as Harris spelled Shogun, was under the influence of six persons or families, which made the rule of Japan seem more an oligarchy than a monarchy to the American. Rumors of negotiations for a commercial treaty with the Dutch reached Harris' ears. But the American put little value in a treaty with the Dutch, who in his opinion were "altogether too fond of monopolies to make a treaty suited to the present wants of the commercial world." Harris was assured by Moriyama that Japan would be opened to foreigners within the year.

In the beginning the Japanese did not quite understand Harris' diplomatic position. What was the difference between his dealings with the officials at Shimoda and his desire to meet with the councilors of the Shogun in Edo? Moriyama tried to find the answer by posing a hypothetical question, which he had "dreamed." "Suppose the Governors of Shimoda should wish to make a commercial treaty with you, what would you do?" was the "dream" question. Harris answered that he would first examine the powers of the officials, and if they were satisfactory, he would show his own and they could all then get to work and make the treaty. This cleared some of the misunderstanding, because it had been believed before that Harris would deal only with the Bakufu in Edo.

Harris explained again that two different matters were involved, which ought not to be confused. One was the treaty; the other was the confidential material from the government of the United States, which could only be revealed in Edo, and the letter from the President of the United States, which could only be delivered in the presence of the Emperor.

Still waiting for word from Edo, Harris continued to observe the novel world of Japan, the traditional days for changing the clothing of one season for its successor's, the twelve-year cycle, the division of the days and the marking of the hours. As May rolled around Harris had been in Japan for eight months and in all that time not one word had reached him from the United States government in Washington. Not a single Navy ship had put in to Shimoda to pay him a call. Hong Kong was only nine days away by steamer, but on May 5 he wrote: "I am more isolated than any American official in any part of the world. I have important intelligence to send to my government—intelligence that will give an immediate spur to our trade with Japan; yet here it remains, month after month, without my being able to communicate it to my government, or enabling my countrymen to benefit by it. The absence of a man-of-war also tends to weaken my influence with the Japanese. They have yielded nothing except from *fear,* any future ameliorations of our intercourse will only take place after a demonstration of force on our part."

All alone except for his secretary, he had to deal with the minor irritations of overcharging tradesmen and the major anxiety of the Japanese government's snail-like pace. Once in a while his patience would be exploded, as on May 26 when he entered in his journal: "They do not regard the promise they gave me last August as worth the breath it cost to utter it. However, to *lie* is, for a Japanese, simply to speak."

To add to his exasperation, May 1857 was a month of raw winds and interminable rain. The weather was bad beyond the memory of the oldest inhabitant of Shimoda, he wrote. Harris was continuously ill, praying for the arrival of a foreign ship with a good doctor. By the end of the month he estimated that he had walked for exercise over three hundred and fifty miles. He had given up tobacco, reduced his diet to plain boiled rice and a little fowl.

In late June the officials in Shimoda were provided with another maneuver: an order from the Shogun's government, under "seal and signature royal," commanding them to receive the letter from the President of the United States and to bring it to Edo. To their absolute amazement, Harris flatly refused. He was not bowled over by the regal paraphernalia of the document. About the same time, June 23, word reached Harris that the second American consul to Japan, E. E. Rice, had arrived at the northern port of Hakodate and "hoisted his flag." The Fourth of July came around and Harris, at a cost of less than two dollars, arranged a national salute of twenty-one guns to honor Independence Day. But he confided in his journal:

"I never felt more miserable and wretched than on this day. Ill in health, in want of everything but low spirits, of which I have an abundant supply. Dear New York! How I wish I could pass the day there among friends."

The summer months dragged on. Harris had been in Japan for a full year plus three days when on September 7, 1857, he met with the Magistrate of Shimoda and to his surprise was informed that the Japanese government had yielded on every point that he had sought: he was to proceed to Edo with full honors and ceremonies; he was to have an immediate meeting with the head of the Council of State; and on the first auspicious day he would have a public audience with the Shogun, at which time he could deliver the letter from the President of the United States.

The following day was another glad day for Harris. An American sloop-of-war, the *Portsmouth,* put in a welcome appearance, despite the news that the *San Jacinto,* with all of Harris' mail, had been at Shanghai for three months, only seven days' journey away, and had never moved to bring him his dispatches and supplies. Harris managed to replenish some of his dwindling provisions from the *Portsmouth* before it departed with the mail and diplomatic dispatches for Washington. But the ship did not carry away the American diplomat, who the commodore of the *San Jacinto* thought might need rescuing from his lonely post.

Harris plunged into the arrangements for his journey to Edo, which would take place within two months. There was no question of the American diplomat "knocking his head" on the floor before the Shogun. The salutation would be the usual one—three bows. Harris insisted that the journey must be at his discretion, with the escort under his command. He was going—not being taken—to the Japanese capital, although he reassured the Japanese that he would be happy to comply with appropriate suggestions. The American retinue consisted of two Westerners: Harris and his secretary, Henry Heusken. In addition there were two Japanese house servants and some forty porters to carry luggage, cooking utensils, bedding and all other supplies for the trip. All Harris' retainers would wear the arms of the United States on their dress.

A month before the journey to Edo got under way, Harris learned that the ruler in the capital was to be called not the shogun ("generalissimo") but *taicun* (tycoon), which meant "great ruler." This information irked Harris, who for more than a year had spoken and written *ziogoon* without being corrected. "The genius of the people shines out in this," he wrote in irritation.

But Harris' health had improved tremendously by the time he and his party set out for Edo early in the morning of November 23. He was on horseback, the morning was fine and the feeling of success made his spirits soar. The American flag was carried before him, and Harris admitted considerable honest pride in showing it in a country that had been isolated for so long. The journey of over a hundred miles overland from Shimoda to Edo would take a week. Over mountainous areas too rugged for his horse, Harris climbed into his sedan chair. He found this conveyance less comfortable. On the second day he had his first view of Mount Fuji, which in the beginning he considered "grand beyond description." Enroute he stopped to visit temples. He was surprised at the hordes of Japanese people who had come, some more than a hundred miles, he was told, to see him pass. The crowds were perfectly behaved; there was no shouting and no noise; all knelt and cast down their eyes as the American passed; only some personages of special rank were permitted to salute him by "knocking head" —actually touching the forehead to the ground.

The procession entered the district of Edo through the village of Hakone, where it was the long established custom for every incoming and outgoing sedan chair to be searched and for every person's passport to be examined. Harris, as a foreign diplomat, would not permit himself or his *norimono* to be searched, even as a token formality.

By the end of the week the American procession had reached Kanagawa, where Commodore Perry had signed the treaty three years before. Across the bay from the village of Yokohama Harris could see three ships of European cut and

Procession of young noblemen, by Hishikawa Moronobu
(Art Institute of Chicago: Clarence Buckingham Collection)

two schooners lying at anchor. These, purchased from the Dutch, were the beginnings of the Japanese navy. Off Kanagawa Harris saw a steamer that had been a gift to Japan from the Dutch.

Without realizing, apparently, the extent of the precautions taken by the Japanese government to insure his safety on the journey, Harris registered the presence of bodies of policemen, carrying iron rods six feet long. Each rod had attached to it four or five iron rings which gave off a jingling sound as the policeman struck the ground with the metal staff. The American was not fully aware of the hostility of many of the feudal lords and some of their more reckless retainers, the *ronin,* or "wave men."

The crowds appeared peaceful to Harris:

"The number of people seen increases. They are all fat, well clad and happy looking, but there is an equal absence of any appearance of wealth or of poverty—a state of things that *may* perhaps constitute the real happiness of a people. I sometimes doubt whether the opening of Japan to foreign influences will promote the *general happiness* of this people. It is more like the golden age of simplicity and honesty than I have ever seen in any other country."

Monday, November 30, 1857, was the day of Townsend Harris' entry into Edo. "It will form an important epoch in my life, and a still more important one in the history of Japan," he wrote. "I am the first diplomatic representative that has ever been received in this city; and, whether I succeed or fail in my intended negotiations, it is a *great fact* that will always remain, showing that at last I have forced this singular people to acknowledge the *rights of embassy*. I feel no little pride, too, in carrying the American Flag through that part of

Bowing before a daimyō procession; print by Ando Hiroshige (Courtesy, Museum of Fine Arts, Boston)

Japan between the extremity of Cape Izu and into the very castle of the City of Edo."

Harris would have preferred to make his entry into the city on horseback, but he chose to be carried in in his uncomfortable sedan chair because he learned that only princes of the highest rank were entitled to enter the city in this fashion. All others could come in either mounted or on foot. Passing along the harbor, he made a note of the mud flats which filled the whole upper part of the bay. It would prevent the approach of large vessels nearer than six miles, he estimated, supposing that Commodore Perry would have discovered the shallows if he had sent his surveying parties just two miles farther up the bay.

Inside Edo, the train of the Americans passed over seven bridges, including the "Bridge of Japan," from which all distances in the country were measured. The entourage moved slowly down seven miles of streets, lined with crowds five deep, which Harris estimated numbered one hundred and eighty thousand persons. Here the people no longer knelt or averted their eyes. There was an endless changing of officials, many wearing the two swords of the samurai, who exhibited a constant "knocking of heads." The vast multitude stood in perfect order and absolute silence. Not a shout, not a cry was heard; to Harris the silence had "something appalling" in it.

A mile from his official residence in Edo, Harris' bearers started carrying him at a full run and rushed him in his sedan chair through a gateway, across a court and into the house— all according to the most honorable Japanese custom. Every effort seemed to have been made to make the American comfortable. The envoy and his secretary were given several rooms each in one of the more imposing buildings inside "the castle," a series of buildings in circles, in the center of which was the residence of the Shogun. Harris' friend, Shinano-no-kami, Magistrate of Shimoda, was on hand to greet him and to conduct him to his quarters. Great relief was expressed that the journey had not been marred by any incident. The Shogunate had been under great anxiety to prevent any trouble. Only the strictest orders had kept people "by the millions," Harris was told, from rushing to the capital to gape at the Westerners.

Harris was received by the head of the Senior Council, who had just taken on the responsibility for Japan's foreign affairs. He was Masayoshi Hotta, a pleasant and intelligent-looking man of about thirty-five. The meeting was ceremonious but without military display. Harris' simple speech to the Shogun was translated and the Shogun's reply was transmitted to the American diplomat. The audience with the Shogun was set for the following Monday, December 7, 1857.

On the appointed day Harris dressed in a coat embroidered with gold and blue and in blue trousers decorated with a broad stripe of gold on each leg. He put on a cocked hat with gold tassels and carried a pearl-handled dress sword. He was conducted inside to a great hall where about three hundred *daimyō* and princes sat like statues, all dressed in formal court attire, all faced in the same direction. The audience chamber itself was just off the great hall, but it was curtained off so that the Japanese noblemen could hear but could not see what was going on before the exalted ruler. Harris' host—or as he sometimes referred to him, "his keeper," entered the audience chamber on his hands and knees. As a chamberlain announced him in a loud voice, Harris entered the audience room, stopped about six feet inside and bowed. He then moved forward until he was opposite Hotta and the five members of the Rōjū, all of whom were prostrate on the floor. On the other side of the room three other figures were prostrate in the same manner. They were the Japanese noblemen who were called the Shogun's brothers.

The Shogun was seated on a chair on a platform raised about two feet above the floor. In front of him a grass curtain hung from the ceiling; it cut off Harris' view of the ruler's head, hiding his headdress. Afterward Harris was told that the curtain had been rolled down too far because the American's height had been misjudged. Before him everyone granted an audience had been obliged to approach the Shogun on his knees.

After the slightest of pauses, Harris delivered an address to the Shogun:

"May it please Your Majesty:

"In presenting my letters of credence from the President of the United States, I am directed to express to Your Majesty the sincere wishes of the President for your health and happiness and for the prosperity of your dominions. I consider it a great honor that I have been selected to fill the high and important place of Plenipotentiary of the United States at the Court of Your Majesty; and, as my earnest wishes are to unite the two countries more closely in the ties of enduring friendship, my constant exertions shall be directed to the attainment of that happy end."

At that point Harris stopped and bowed once more. The Shogun responded firmly with a pleasant voice:

"Pleased with the letter sent with Ambassador from a distant country, and likewise pleased with his discourse.

"Intercourse shall be continued forever."

Harris' secretary, who had been carrying the letter from President Pierce, now stepped into the audience chamber, bowing three times. Harris removed the silk cover and displayed the letter so that the writing could be seen. Hotta had stood up to receive the letter in its handsome container, which he placed on a lacquered stand. The Japanese councilor then resumed his position on his knees. The Shogun made Harris a slight bow, indicating that the audience was at an end. In response Harris bowed, stepped backward, bowed again and then for the last time, ending the historic meeting.

When Harris got back to his official lodgings, he was seriously ill, his lungs inflamed, his body shaking with a violent ague. The next day, still ill, Harris sent word to Hotta that he had some important messages either for his ears or for the entire Rōjū. The following Saturday, December 12, the American and the Japanese statesman met again and conversed for two hours. Harris described the changing world outside of Japan and pointed out that sooner or later Japan would have to surrender her policy of isolation, and that, far from suffering because of it, the empire and her people would grow prosperous. Harris told Hotta that the nations of the world would continue to knock at the gates of Japan, sending armed fleets if necessary to demand access to the country. Even if open warfare could be avoided, Japan would suffer endless panics and alarms because of the presence of powerful foreign vessels in its harbors. The American showed the Japanese councilor that a treaty made with an ambassador would be much more generous than an agreement forced on the country by an armed fleet. It became evident that if the Japanese government had to yield to force what it would not give freely, it would weaken its power and prestige.

Recording his conference with Hotta in his journal, Harris said:

"I told him that, by negotiating with me who had purposely come to Edo alone and without the presence of even a single man-of-war, the honor of Japan would be saved; that each point would be carefully discussed and that the country should be gradually opened.

"I added that the three great points would be: 1st, the reception of foreign ministers to reside at Edo; 2nd, the freedom to trade with the Japanese without the interference of Government officers; and 3rd, the opening of additional harbors."

Harris assured the Japanese counselor that he was not asking exclusive rights for the United States, but he pointed out that terms accepted by the President would become acceptable to all the other Western powers.

"I did not fail to point out the danger to Japan of having opium forced upon her, and said I would be willing to prohibit the bringing it to Japan."

The Japanese kept even more careful notes of the statements made that day by Harris to Hotta.

They showed Harris explaining how the electric telegraph has made rapid communication possible between distant points, that steam made California and Japan only eighteen days apart, that commerce was expanding and that no nation had the right to hold itself aloof. Harris was pictured reporting the dangers of war the Japanese faced in the rivalries between Russia and England, both of whom wanted naval bases in the northern Japanese islands. As an example, he pointed to the state of affairs in China, which had lost a million people in a war with England and had, in addition, been forced to pay millions of pounds as an indemnity to reestablish peace. In addition, Chinese cities had been destroyed, the country's defenses weakened, and worse, opium had been brought in from India, a traffic estimated by Harris at twenty-five million dollars yearly. Harris is described in the Japanese notes as calling opium "the one great enemy of China." "If it is used it weakens the body and injures it like the most deadly poison; it makes the rich poor and the wise foolish; it unmans all that use it, and by reason of the misery it brings, robbers and acts of violence increase." Harris reported that the United States considered opium "more dangerous than war" and was prepared to outlaw it.

"The President [of the United States] is of the opinion," Harris was reported as saying to Hotta, "that if Japan makes a treaty with the United States, all other foreign countries will make the same kind of a treaty, and Japan will be safe thereafter.

"The President wants to make a treaty that will be honorable to Japan, without war, in a peaceable manner, after deliberate consultation. If Japan should make a treaty with the ambassador of the United States, who has come unattended by military force, her honor will not be impaired. There will be a great difference between a treaty made with a single individual, unattended, and one made with a person, who should bring fifty men-of-war to these shores."

Harris then told Hotta that as soon as the war with China, then going on, was ended, the English governor at Hong Kong planned to bring the largest fleet ever seen to Edo to force the admission of a British ambassador and the opening of trade. The French ambassador wrote Harris that as soon as the Chinese war was over, he too was coming with fifty steamers.

"The best-informed people think the Chinese war cannot last long; hence the English ambassador may be expected before long," Harris predicted.

"If I write in my name to the agents of England and France residing in Asia and inform them that Japan is ready to make a commercial treaty with their countries, the number of steamers will be reduced from fifty to two or three."

Harris stayed on in Edo for several months, spending many

hours in careful explanations to the Japanese about diplomatic usages between countries and business procedures and regulations. The Japanese asked for the same explanations over and over, admitting that they were unfamiliar with so many modern concepts. Harris complied with the utmost patience. Many ideas of political economy and international business

Norimono *and bearers; print by Hishikawa Moronobu (Courtesy, Museum of Fine Arts, Boston: Ross Collection)*

were so new to the Japanese that they had no word for them.
The corresponding Dutch terms were also incomprehensible
and it took great effort to convey the simplest notion. The
Japanese listened carefully to all the explanations, which were
immediately rediscussed in the highest government councils,
Harris believed. It was fortunate that the American diplomat

enjoyed the full confidence of the Japanese. He handed them a written memorandum, which he said could be the basis for a commercial treaty. The Japanese undertook to give it the most careful study.

Christmas Day 1857 was spent in Edo. "Merry Christmas!" Harris wrote in his journal. "I little thought on last Christmas to pass the present one in Edo. If I could pass one in Pekin, it would make my different places of passing the day a remarkable list."

The discussions inside Japan that began after Commodore Perry's first visit in 1853 were continuing with ever more intensity. The new trade, the residence of foreign diplomats in Japan, even the power and effectiveness of the Shogunate, were debated fiercely. The general opinion did not favor ending the country's isolation.

Late in December, in an effort to win as much support as possible for inevitable changes, Hotta asked for fuller discussions of Japan's foreign policy. He set forth his estimate of the situation confronting his country and summarized the two prevailing views about "the way in which the foreigners should be treated"

The first sought to gain time to build up Japan's military strength with which to drive the foreigners out, meanwhile temporizing with trade agreements and postponing conflict year by year. The second view was even more defiant, saying that "no matter how many thousands of warships the foreigners may send," Japan should unite its strength and go to war at once.

Hotta's opinion was that "neither of these views is apt to the present state of affairs. Nor do they hold out any prospect of ultimate success. One inclines to procrastination, one relies on violence, and both alike would lead us astray. Of recent times a change has come over world conditions in general. All countries are alike in concluding treaties by which they make friendly alliances, open trade, exchange their products and help each other in difficulties. Hence not to enter into friendly relations entails war and not to wage war entails entering into friendly relations; there is no other way, and there is not a single country which avoids both friendly relations and war, which spurns diplomacy and yet enjoys peace and maintains its independence. . . . I am therefore convinced that our policy should be to stake everything on the present opportunity, to conclude friendly alliances, to send ships to foreign countries everywhere and conduct trade, to copy the foreigners where they are at their best and so repair our own shortcomings, to foster our national strength and to complete our armaments, and so gradually subject the foreigners to our influence, until in the end all the countries of the world know the blessings of perfect tranquility, and our hegemony is acknowledged throughout the globe. From the dawn of history our country has always preserved one Imperial line unbroken, has observed the proper distinction between ruler and subject, between high and low, and has held an enlightened moral code. And although ours is a small country, its land is fertile, its population much denser than that of other countries, and it cherishes a spirit of resoluteness and valor. Once we have laid the foundations of national wealth and strength, therefore, it will be by no means impossible for us to accomplish thereafter the great task of uniting all the world. We must fix our eyes on that objective."

One of the major opponents of any and all intercourse with the West was Nariaki Tokugawa, a member of the Shogun's family, who responded with horror at the idea of a foreigner living in Edo. He suggested a novel alternative: that he would go to America with three or four hundred unwanted younger sons, pardoned criminals and exiles, and he would act as a middleman to carry on trade with America. Other Japanese could be sent, in similar manner, to any other country that wanted to trade with Japan. "It would place Japan in extreme danger if the government were to allow foreigners to enter Edo," he wrote to the Rōjū.

Other reports to the Rōjū stressed the importance of keeping the foreigners out of Edo and also out of the city of Osaka, which was too close to Kyoto. One Japanese nobleman expressed his view "that if the Bakufu grants these points (to open trade and to set up an embassy in Edo), then no matter what sort of agreement is made now, the boundless greed of the foreigners will certainly bring more and greater demands hereafter. Nor will the matter end with America alone. The Bakufu will have to grant privileges on the same footing to other foreigners as well, and all sorts of difficulties will arise."

The last writer offered a sly suggestion that the Japanese government accept Harris' offers of friendship and commerce, but hold everything off until both countries felt the need *at the same time* to dispatch ministers to each other's capitals. He strongly implied that Japan would be a long time feeling the need.

In 1853, following Commodore Perry's first visit, a young Japanese nobleman had called for immediate preparations for war. Five years later Keiei Matsudaira seemed to have broadened his outlook, though some of his objectives remained the same. His response to the proposed commercial treaty was:

"To men of discernment, I believe, it is quite clear that present conditions make national seclusion impossible.

"It is most desirable that we should begin the practice of navigation and visit other countries in search of trade. The

Bakufu, therefore, should not refuse those who come and present their demands reasonably and should reply similarly concerning the question of 'ministers'.

"A wealthy country is the basis of military strength. It is therefore my desire that we should henceforward establish a commercial system and begin the study of trade. We should engage in the exchange of products and thus take advantage of our country's geographical advantages to make her the richest country in the world.

"Since commerce depends on the circulation of money, however, there is a danger that such a plan may in fact give rise to luxury and weakness within Japan.

"Again, in these critical times, the fact that there are dangerous tendencies in public feeling at home and that our customs differ from those of the foreigners might cause a serious crisis at any moment. Nor do I believe that the mere presence or absence of a minister could determine whether or no we should suffer the same fate as overtook China in the Opium War.

"The thing most to be feared is not the influx of other countries, but the rivalry between England and Russia. The fact that these two Powers cannot coexist has been made abundantly clear by the envoy's statement. That one of these two might sometime seek privileges that would inevitably endanger the State is the thought that fills me with the greatest concern.

"In dominating men or being dominated by them, the issue turns simply on the question of who has the initiative. I believe that in present conditions this is our chief problem.

"That being so, rather than sitting idly awaiting the coming attack of the foreign countries, we should construct innumerable warships, annex neighbouring small territories, and foster commerce. By so doing we will in fact accomplish deeds far excelling those of European countries, will in the end make glorious for ever our country's honoured name and shatter the selfish designs of the brutish foreigners. This alone is my cherished wish.

"In this connexion, the Bakufu will never be able to achieve success by means of the traditional policy it has so far pursued in domestic affairs. The essential and first action to be taken, as I have recommended before, is to nominate a man of genuine ability as successor to the Shōgun. Then the services of capable men must be enlisted from the entire country; peacetime extravagance must be cut down and the military system revised; the evil practices by which the *daimyō* and lesser lords have been impoverished must be discontinued; preparations must be made both on land and sea, not only in the main islands but also in Ezo; the daily livelihood of the whole people must be fostered; and schools for the various arts and crafts must be established.

"These are important and weighty matters, but the time has come when radical reforms must be carried out. Moreover, the American requests have been stated clearly and reasonably. The Bakufu should therefore inform the envoy that it intends to put these recommendations into effect and should question him closely concerning conditions abroad. After carefully considering what he says, we should seek the views of the Emperor and zealously put this policy into operation. By so doing, I believe, we shall find that here and now we have the opportunity of revolutionizing our fortunes. I cannot explain in so short a letter how this is to be carried out in detail, but if you should be so good as to ask me to do so, I will speak frankly and without reserve. I sincerely desire that you will give close attention to the various ideas I have advanced.

"Submitted with respect."

Disagreement inside Japan was becoming more and more violent. The country was rushing toward civil war. What Harris heard as lying by the Japanese negotiators was more properly a frantic effort to stall for time. The Japanese temporized, waiting for some united opinion to develop. Perhaps they also hoped that the American might eventually give up in despair and go away.

The New Year, 1858, found Harris in Edo, still waiting while the Japanese ministers and noblemen discussed and debated the propositions he had put before them. No word of all these deliberations was reported to the American, whose patience was being severely tested. Edo was shaken by earthquakes, which he dutifully noted in his journal. His Japanese hosts came to pay him New Year's Day calls and brought him presents of cloths and lacquers but not the answer he wanted to hear so eagerly. After twenty-nine days of waiting Harris decided to bring matters to a head. Early in January he confronted the Japanese with the blunt statement that unless he was given some indication that he could expect a reply of some sort within a specified time, he was heading back to Shimoda, considering himself and the President of the United States insulted by the offhand treatment.

Harris reassured himself about "this apparently bold step." "From my knowledge of this people," he wrote, "I felt that I ran no kind of danger of breaking off my negotiations by what I did, and that the more I yielded and acquiesced, the more they would impose on me, while, by taking a bold attitude and assuming a threatening tone, I should at once bring them to terms."

The Japanese reacted immediately much as Harris predicted. He was informed that the matter was being discussed by the highest nobility of the land, by the feudal lords, the military and literary classes, but that regardless he would have a reply by the following Thursday, January 15.

"This was much to my satisfaction," he wrote in his journal on January 11. "And I told the Prince [of Shinano] that, so long as I had specific days fixed, then I could wait with patience."

Harris had a second interview with Hotta, where he was informed that his proposals for the residence of foreign ambassadors in Edo would be accepted, that the right of free trade would be granted to the diplomatic agents, but that more harbors in Japan could not be opened for foreign access. The details of the accepted proposals would be worked out by negotiation, Harris was told. But the American protested the decision not to open additional harbors, pointing out that Japan's coastline was longer than most other countries and that for a thousand miles along the Japan Sea not a harbor was available.

Two commissioners were appointed by the Japanese to start the negotiations with Harris. One was his friend, Inouye, Shinano-no-kami, Magistrate of Shimoda; the other was Iwase, Higo-no-kami. Harris knew that the commissioners, in reality, would report every word to the Great Council where every question would be fully considered. Arrangements to begin meeting were made immediately.

Harris had prepared a draft treaty before leaving Shimoda, and he immediately offered it to the Japanese commissioners once their official powers had been exchanged. The American was anxious to keep the initiative in presenting written documents on which to base the treaty because he knew that once a Japanese language draft appeared, it would be difficult if not impossible to reject it entirely. "To try to amend one of their performances would have made a piece of literary or diplomatic patchwork that would have excited the laughter of all who might have the misfortune to be compelled to read it," he explained in his notebook.

Serious negotiations for a treaty between the United States and Japan were commenced on Monday, January 25. In his notes for that important day, Harris commented:

"I shall confine myself to the main leading facts of actual transactions, omitting the interminable discourse of the Japanese where the same proposition may be repeated a dozen times; nor shall I note their positive refusal of points they subsequently grant, and mean to grant all the while; nor many absurd proposals made by them without the hope, and scarcely the wish, of having them accepted—for all such proceedings are according to the rule of Japanese diplomacy, and he who shows the greatest absurdity in such matters is most esteemed.

"They do not know the value of a straightforward and truthful policy, at least they do not practice it. They never hesitate uttering a falsehood even where truth would serve the same purpose."

Harris, for example, did not believe the story of a threat to his life which the commissioners reported at their first meeting. To the American it was too pat and too coincidental because it was advanced as a reason for keeping foreign ambassadors out of Edo. The story of the commissioners concerned the dispossessed and masterless bully-boys, the *ronin*, or wave men, who wandered through the countryside, sometimes with one *daimyō,* sometimes with another. The *ronin* regarded the presence of a foreign diplomat in the Japanese capital as some sort of national disgrace and a plot to harm Harris had been uncovered in time, according to the Japanese commissioners. The American negotiator, unaware that the threat was serious and real, would not be swayed from his insistence on the right of residence in Edo.

In the midst of the negotiations Harris often was surprised

to learn new facts about Japan which he had beforehand taken for granted. He heard that the Imperial capital of Japan was called Kyoto, not Miaco, which was just a Japanese word meaning capital. The information nettled Harris, who jotted down a parenthetical note in his record of the day's negotiations.

"This is another instance of the extraordinary secretiveness of the Japanese; for more than three hundred years they have permitted foreigners to call it Miako, instead of Kyoto!"

Among other things that were brought to his attention were:

"The merchants and common people are no doubt in favor of opening the country, but the daimyō and the military oppose it."

The reaction of the Shogun's negotiators to the Emperor in Kyoto was recorded in another parenthesis:

"They spoke almost contemptuously of the Mikado, and roared with laughter when I quoted some remarks concerning the veneration in which he is held by the Japanese. They say he has neither money, political power, nor anything else that is valued in Japan. He is a mere cipher."

At the very same time, however, the Shogunate decided it would be an advantage to get the Emperor's consent to the proposed treaty with the United States. A special ambassador to "the Spiritual Power" had been sent to Kyoto to convince the Emperor and obtain his approval. The special ambassador was Hayashi, Lord Rector of the University, who could bring all his experience negotiating with Commodore Perry to help him explain to the Imperial Court why Japan had to open its doors to the West. Hayashi could not overcome the conserva-

Wave men, or ronin; *scene from a play, by Katsushika Hokusai (Courtesy, Museum of Fine Arts, Boston: Bigelow Collection)*

tive influence over the Emperor, which violently rejected any dealings with foreign barbarians.

A second ambassador went to Kyoto, this time Hotta himself. There was such intense disagreement, even among the Shogun's followers, that the agreement of the Emperor, it was hoped, would bring around the most stubborn of the diehards. Harris inquired what would happen if the Emperor refused his consent. The Shogunate had "determined not to receive any objections from the Mikado," he was told. But even the chief minister in person could not overcome the opposition of the Emperor and his court, who wanted no changes in the country's centuries-old traditions. Support for the agreement with the West was limited: only four of the eighteen great *daimyō* favored the treaty, Harris learned, while only a hundred or more of the lesser feudal lords were in accord. The Shogunate was doing its utmost to bring around the unwilling majority.

These embassies to the Emperor in Kyoto and the flaring opposition to the treaty prompted the Japanese to propose a delay in signing the document. Harris did not want to be put off but he had to compromise. He suggested that the treaty be completely worked out and prepared for signature, but that the Japanese government send him a written message indicating that the ceremony of signing would be postponed for sixty days. Harris intended to use the time to prepare his reports to the United States Government. Hotta sent the letter to Harris, pledging the faith of the Japanese government.

The month of conferences had produced agreement on the following questions: an American "diplomatic agent" would be permitted to reside in Edo and American consuls would live at any or all of the ports opened to American commerce. These ports were to be, in addition to Shimoda and Hakodate, which had been agreed upon with Perry, the ports and towns of Kanagawa (to be opened on July 4, 1859), Nagasaki (also July 4, 1859), Niigata (January 1, 1860) and Hyogo (modern Kobe, on January 1, 1863). Shimoda was to be closed down six months after the opening of Kanagawa. American diplomats and consuls were granted the right to travel freely in Japan. American businessmen and others were to be permitted to lease ground, build homes and warehouses, but not to arm or fortify them.

Rights to reside in Edo for the purpose of commerce would be given from January 1, 1862, and in Osaka, on January 1, 1863. Trading was made free of government interference and opened to all classes of Japanese. The treaty permitted Americans to move about freely except for certain limits at Kanagawa, Hakodate and Hyogo. The Imperial capital of Kyoto was not to be approached nearer than ten Japanese *ri,* about twenty-five miles. Freedom of worship was guaranteed and the privileges accorded of building suitable places of worship.

By the terms of the treaty, Japan was empowered to name an ambassador to Washington and to appoint consuls for any or all ports in the United States, with the right to travel wherever they wished in any part of the country.

As he had suggested from the outset, Harris agreed that "the importation of opium" by American vessels would not be allowed, and that the Japanese had the right to seize and destroy any surplus of opium over four pounds found on any American ship in a Japanese harbor.

The negotiations continued through February until agreement was reached on all the articles of the treaty. A final draft was prepared and sent to Japanese Rōjū, where it was weighed until the first days of March. During the same period, the debate inside Japan continued with mounting intensity. Early in May, Hotta was summoned to the Emperor's palace in Kyoto to hear the Imperial orders that the Shogunate reconsider its course—that is, reject the American draft treaty. The Emperor's instructions were explicit:

"The American affair is a great sorrow to our divine land and a matter truly vital to the safety of the State. The Em-

peror keenly feels his responsibility in this to his Imperial An-
cestry, most of all those enshrined at Ise. He greatly fears
that to revolutionize the sound laws handed down from the
time of Ieyasu [first of the Tokugawa Shoguns] would disturb

*Warriors guarding the Emperor; painting attributed to Tosa
Mitsushige (The Metropolitan Museum of Art, New York:
Bequest of Mrs. H. O. Havemeyer, 1929; The H. O. Havemeyer
Collection)*

the ideas of our people and make it impossible to preserve lasting tranquility. The treaty opening the port of Shimoda some years ago was serious enough, but it is the Emperor's belief that the provisional treaty now proposed would make impossible the preservation of national honor."

There were other complicating factors. The ruling Shogun Iesada was in failing health and without direct male heirs. Sharp rivalries sprang up between Tokugawa branch houses, dividing the loyalties of potential successors. But on July 27 Townsend Harris rushed back to Kanagawa with the news that the war in China was over, with the English and French fleets victorious. A joint Anglo-French expedition against Japan could be expected momentarily. Harris urged the Japanese to sign the treaty with the United States without delay. If they did not, they might have to start from the beginning under the guns of the combined English and French fleets.

The Japanese commissioners reported Harris' message to the Rōjū, which was hastily called into session on July 29. In spite of the Emperor's disapproval, the State Council and the new Great Councilor, Naosuke Ii, instructed the negotiators to sign the treaty since there seemed no other course. That day the "Treaty of Amity and Commerce between the United States and Japan" was signed aboard Perry's old flagship, the *Mississippi,* anchored in Edo Bay. The two commissioners signed for Japan and for the United States the signature affixed was Townsend Harris.

In August 1858, the thirteenth Shogun of the Tokugawa line, Iesada, died. In November, the fourteenth Tokugawa Shogun, Iemochi, took power in Edo.

The opposition to the treaty with America continued, particularly in Kyoto at the Imperial Court. Toward the end of

1858, Akikatsu Manabe, spokesman for the Bakufu, reported to the Kampaku, senior official of the Emperor's court:

"I have the honour to acknowledge receipt of the Imperial instructions. It was stated therein that [while] the Emperor [Kōmei] . . . recognized that the Bakufu had acted as it did by force of circumstance, his views on the subject had not in any way changed since last spring; and were he to permit our people to mix with the foreigners and to allow trade and trading posts, though it be but for a single day, to say nothing of five or six years, this would be to contradict the announcement he made in July last when he sent lords to Ise [Great Shrine of Imperial Family] as his envoys and would cause him the deepest concern. . . .

"I have already fully explained that, facing as we were difficulties both at home and abroad, the Bakufu had no choice but to sign the treaties. Perhaps the Court does not fully appreciate this fact. I am told the Emperor has in no way changed his views since last spring and cannot see his way to approving the treaties. Yet the question of how to deal with foreign countries is a crucial one. In the Bakufu, too, there would be much less concern if our action conformed to Imperial commands; and the Shōgun seeks to act in whatever way will serve to carry out the Emperor's wishes, for no matter what the circumstances an Imperial pronouncement is something commanding respect. But there are other considerations, too. With the arrival of the English and French we were faced with a choice between war and peace, and the Shōgun therefore took action in accordance with his hereditary responsibilities. Even so, he is deeply concerned and feels it a matter of the utmost regret that the treaties were signed without reference to the Court. . . .

"As I have said above, not to have signed the treaties would have provoked war. Moreover, to repudiate the treaties after both sides have signed them is equally impossible. You might think that negotiations for cancelling the treaties would be possible on the grounds that they are termed 'provisional' treaties, but the expression 'provisional' does not here have the meaning of 'temporary'. As long as a treaty does not bear the monarch's name and seal it is described as 'provisional', but although it is not yet formally concluded, it is valid from the date of the original agreement.

"More generally, the treaties have been negotiated, agreed, and signed as a result of the Shōgun's decision to adopt a policy of friendship [and all countries believe that the Bakufu possessed the necessary political authority for such action]. Repudiation of the treaties would never be accepted now, no matter what arguments we advanced. As the Emperor's orders now stand, I fear, they are tantamount to ordering repudiation of the treaties and the opening of hostilities. If we disown the treaties we shall be dishonoured, while the reputation of the foreigners will be untouched. All countries would join in branding us faithless and unjust and would send their warships against us. If that happened, our position would indeed be critical. Our preparations in terms of ships and guns are still incomplete. If we plunge thus recklessly into war, not only will we have no prospect for victory, but the domestic tranquility we have known for nearly three hundred years would change to disorder. . . . Where lies the advantage or the wisdom in opening hostilities thus recklessly?

"Even if the Court issued orders that the foreign envoys were to be summoned to Kyōto, the Bakufu would not be able to carry out such orders, for it would not be in the country's interests to do so. This is not a question of America alone. Provisional treaties have also been concluded with Russia, England, France, and Holland. Thus whatever the orders of the

Court may be, to rescind the treaties at this time would be to invite both foreign and domestic dangers at once. To insist on abrogating them would be nothing less than to resolve on war. Yet, as I have already said, our military equipment, in terms of warships and cannon, is still incomplete. The *daimyō* are equally ill equipped with such weapons. [High and low are alike impoverished.] It matters little how courageously our people bear themselves in war. Our opponents have had many years' experience of actual warfare and are amply provided with warships and guns. The five above countries for certain, and probably other countries in alliance with them, would send hundreds of ships against our coast on every side, burning and laying waste. We should be fighting alone. With all countries ranged against us we should not, as things are, have even the means of defending ourselves. Our outlying islands . . . and the seven islands of the Izu group, would be seized by the foreigners; and we might even be unable to protect the Imperial Palace. How great, then, would be the hardships we should inflict on our people! This would truly be the height of inhumanity, a cause of indescribable suffering.

"When finally the war ended and we began to discuss peace terms, we should be forced to bow to their wishes and complete treaties entirely dictated by them, leasing them territory and granting them the right to live among Japanese. In that, we should suffer the same tragic fate as China. Although a large country, China was defeated in war by England and had to conclude a new and revised treaty with her. This treaty, as I have reported separately, followed English ideas. It opened several ports, granted English officials equality of status, authorized English subjects to travel freely throughout the country and if they wished to live among the Chinese outside the treaty-port settlements, and provided that the term 'barbarian' was not to be used in official documents. It certainly contained no such regulations as are to be found in the provisional treaties we have just concluded. Thus there can be no question that if we should ever find ourselves in the same position as China, we should suffer such disgrace as could never be wiped out.

"It is a matter of the utmost regret to us that we cannot now act in accordance with the Imperial will, [but knowing as we do that it would not be in the country's interest to do so, to provoke war none the less and make it impossible for men to dwell in tranquility at home, . . . would be contrary to the purposes for which generations of Shōgun have been entrusted with the responsibilities of government. The Shōgun would be much troubled by it, despite the respect which generations of his predecessors have felt for the Imperial Ancestors]. In the interests of the country as a whole, the Bakufu must respectfully but unremittingly remonstrate against any present opening of hostilities. Were the Emperor to announce that he recognizes that in the circumstances the Bakufu had no choice but to act as it did and that it must so act for the future as to fulfil the Imperial will, then, since those in Edo, too, have always been of this same mind, the Shōgun could act so as to unite Court and Bakufu and thereafter, in the course of time, effect the withdrawal of the foreigners. But it would be most unfortunate were the Imperial instructions to state that the treaty could never be justified to the Imperial Ancestors, most of all those enshrined at Ise, and was contrary to the announcement made in July last when the Emperor sent lords to Ise as his envoys. For some time now the Shōgun has been anxious to act only after making a detailed report on the situation to the Emperor. It is, after all, his wish to show proper respect for the Imperial Court. He is convinced that the Emperor's completely unexpected attitude was due to lack of detailed information concerning foreign affairs. As such, it is most proper and reasonable. There are those, however, who put about exaggerated reports of the foreigners' attitude, calling them haughty, arrogant, and so on. It is generally said, too, that the Emperor's ideas may gradually have been contaminated by these base and idle rumors. [However, full investigation shows that there are some most important persons among those guilty of this great crime; and since we should indeed be jeopardizing the very existence of our country were we now to bring about foreign and domestic conflict simultaneously, the Shōgun is generally willing to overlook what they have done on the assumption that it sprang from misunderstanding. But should it happen that despite what I have been saying it is still not recognized that Bakufu policy is in the true interests of the country, should there still be rebellious talk, then the Shōgun may have to distinguish between right and wrong. In that event, it will indeed become impossible to effect the objects of domestic tranquility and Court-Bakufu unity which the Emperor regards so highly.] And since it would be much to be regretted were the Imperial mind to be further disturbed in this way, we shall investigate carefully and make everything clear to the Court. Investigations are already in progress both in Kyōto and in Edo, and after the strictest and most searching examination a further report will be submitted on this question.

"The question now before us is truly one on which the peace of our country turns. The decision [concerning the treaty] was taken by the Bakufu in accordance with its proper responsibilities; but in that it was signed without reference to the Court, the Shōgun Iesada instructed me to submit detailed explanations to you. I respectfully ask that you will again convey these statements to the Emperor."

In Kyoto, however, the opposition to the American treaty

was unyielding. The cry there had changed to *"Sonnö Jōi!* Honor the Emperor—expel the barbarian."A movement in support of the Emperor was gaining strength. The motives were as much aimed at destroying the Tokugawa Shogunate as at driving out the foreigners. Nariaki Tokugawa had strong influence at the Court, and he expressed his opposition to the new treaty in intemperate terms: the Japanese commissioners should be ordered to commit suicide and Harris should be decapitated. The anti-Shogun forces around Emperor Kōmei, however, were not yet able to confront the Shogun and his government directly. Instead a response was sent to the Bakufu spokesman, Akikatsu Manabe, which read:

"The treaty providing for friendship and trade with foreigners and other matters is a blemish on our Empire and a stain on our divine land. This question caused the Emperor's predecessor [Ninkō] great anxiety and he issued instructions concerning it. The present Emperor [Kōmei] greatly fears that were such things to start in his reign, he would find it truly impossible to justify himself to his Imperial Ancestors, most of all those enshrined at Ise. He has thought much on this and his anxiety concerning it is constant, as you have often been informed since last spring. However, since the recent arrival in the capital of Manabe [Akikatsu] Shimōsa-no-kami and Sakai [Tadayoshi] Wakasa-no-kami, several reports have been submitted to the effect that the Shōgun himself, as well as the Tairō [regent], Rōjū, and other officials, are all in agreement with the Emperor in thinking that we must assuredly keep aloof from foreigners and revert to the sound rule of seclusion as formerly laid down in our national laws. The Emperor was much eased in his mind to learn this.

"Accordingly, we must at all events secure greater unity between Court and Bakufu and so adopt the sound policy of reverting [to seclusion] as described above. The Emperor fully understands that in the circumstances the Bakufu could have done no other than it did; and he will therefore exercise forbearance on this occasion. The Bakufu is enjoined to pay special attention to the coastal areas near Kyōto and the Ise shrines, as was stated the other day, for this is a matter touching the respect due to the sacred Imperial Regalia by which our country is preserved."

Caught between the pressures of the West, with its warships, and the unrelenting opposition centered around the Emperor's Court, the Shogunate tried to escape from its quandary by agreeing secretly to fix a date to expel the Westerners from Japan. It is doubtful that the agreement could ever have been kept.

Early in February of 1859 Joseph Heco, the young Japanese seaman who had gone back to San Francisco seven years before, heard the news that a treaty of friendship and commerce had been signed with his native land and that new ports were to be opened to American trade. Heco had become a naturalized American citizen and was employed as a captain's clerk on a naval surveying schooner. He made immediate arrangements to leave his ship and go back to Japan. He journeyed via Hong Kong and Shanghai, where he was introduced to Townsend Harris, newly appointed minister to Japan and to E. M. Dorr, who had been appointed American consul at Kanagawa. Heco was offered the post of official interpreter to the Kanagawa consulate, which was immediately accepted.

Heco came to Shanghai on the *Powhatan*. He transferred to the *Mississippi*, which was carrying Ambassador Harris and Consul Dorr to Japan. The ship arrived in Nagasaki to take on a supply of coal. A four-day run brought it to Shimoda, where the ship remained until the end of June 1859. Just be-

fore July 4 the American diplomats and their Japanese-American interpreter steamed past Uraga and arrived at Kanagawa. Their presence was announced to the Japanese officials, along with the report that they had come to open the port as provided in the Treaty of 1858.

On the United States's Independence Day Ambassador Harris, Consul Dorr, the officers of the *Mississippi* and Joseph Heco landed to take part in the formal opening of Kanagawa

横濱海道蒸氣鑵車岸圖

*Japanese port, open
to the West;
contemporary print
(Library of Congress)*

to commerce with the West. The American consulate was set
up in a temple, in front of which a tall tree was transformed
into a flagpole. At noon the American colors were run up the
flagstaff. Champagne flowed and everyone joined in singing
the national anthem. The next day Harris moved up to Edo
to establish the American embassy there.

There was some question of locating the foreign settlement,
with the diplomats favoring the treaty site of Kanagawa, but

with traders and businessmen soon preferring the deeper anchorage of Yokohama across the bay. The Japanese officials also wanted to see the foreigners established in Yokohama to protect them from hostile attacks by unreconciled opponents of the treaty. Kanagawa was on the main highroad which was frequently traveled by the feudal *daimyō* of Japan and their retainers. There were also many uncontrollable "wave men." Outraged by the presence of the Western barbarians, they would have liked nothing better than to embroil the Shogunate with the foreign powers by attacking the visiting Westerners.

During the first years of Japan's intercourse with the West there were many outbreaks of violence and murder, both foreigners and Japanese falling victims to fierce hatreds. A Russian naval officer was stabbed to death in Yokohama. Fatal attacks took the lives of servants of the French embassy, Dutch sea captains, the Japanese interpreter at the British Consulate and, in January 1861, of Harris' secretary, Henry Heusken.

The assassination of the Japanese senior councilor, Naosuke Ii, brought to light the impossible promise of the Shogunate to drive out the Westerners by a set date. Ii had been one of the principal supporters of the treaty with the United States.

But by that time, March 1860, Japan's first embassy was on its way to Washington. In May, ratifications of the treaty were exchanged in Washington and on the twenty-third of the month it was officially proclaimed in effect. Japan had opened its doors to the world.

EPILOGUE

The opening of Japan to commerce with the West in 1858 was not, of course, the end of the story.

Inside Japan the bitterness over the admission of the hated foreigner mounted for ten years. Many of the Japanese nobility and old landed feudal aristocracy began to rally around the long-neglected Imperial throne in Kyoto. After centuries of submission, the lords of the southern and western provinces saw a chance to unseat their Tokugawa rivals.

In Kyoto the 120th Emperor, Kōmei, on the throne since 1846, was succeeded in 1867 by his son, Meiji. The following year the Shogunate was overthrown and the rule of the Japanese Imperial house restored. Japan's capital was transferred to Edo, which was renamed Tokyo.

The diehard forces which had violently opposed the Shogunate and its traffic with the West, however, found themselves soon repudiated by the Imperial government. The new young Emperor's advisers, realizing the advantage of Western ties, established even stronger relations with all international powers.

The central figures on the American side of the story were treated more honorably by their country. In New York Commodore Perry, having finished the work on the monumental three-volume *Narrative of the Expedition of an American Naval Squadron to the China Seas and Japan,* caught a severe cold and died on March 4, 1858. He was buried with his country's highest honors.

Townsend Harris, suffering continuous ill health, resigned as Minister Resident of the United States in Japan when Abraham Lincoln was elected President. Lincoln accepted the resignation "with profound regret." Harris died in New York in 1878 at the age of seventy-four.

In the twentieth century Japan has been both the ally and the enemy of the United States. In World War I (1914–18) Japan fought against Germany on the side of the United States, England and France. But in the Second World War (1939–45) Japan was the partner of Germany and Italy and an enemy of the United States and the Allies. The historic anniversary of Townsend Harris' audience with the Shogun has been overshadowed by another occasion eighty-four years later to the day, December 7, 1941: Japan's attack on Pearl Harbor, which began World War II in the Pacific.

Nagasaki, for so many centuries the only port of entry for Westerners in Japan, was the last Japanese city to be attacked by the United States in the Second World War. Nagasaki was hit by the second atom bomb, dropped on August 9, 1945. Japan surrendered on August 10.

In the first hundred years following Commodore Perry's historic mission, Japan welcomed Western ideas and Western methods. It quickly mastered the latest innovations in science, technology, industry and finance, and became one of the leading commercial nations of the world. But in spite of apparent westernization, the Japanese have not abandoned their own individuality as an Eastern people.

During that same century the West came to see Japan as more than a coaling station and a commercial market. Japanese art reached Europe and immediately exerted profound influences on Western painting. Japanese silks, porcelains and lacquers became known throughout the world. Japanese thought and culture attracted enthusiastic admirers.

The next chapters in the story that began with a Portuguese adventurer in the middle of the sixteenth century and an American merchantman selling otter fur at the end of the eighteenth are probably already being written by the younger generations of many countries. A friendly exchange of letters between two students, American and Japanese, contains a hint of the questions and answers facing both. The Japanese youth wrote to his American friend:

"Our ancestors had lived alone as Japanese for the long time. But suddenly *impolite* foreign country insisted on opening gate by their right named force. . . . Japan was the last East. But the unreasonable action insisted and insist on us being Western. But we can't be so fast. So we are Eastern in a part, in another part we must be Western. So we can't be Eastern nor Western. That is the gap between Japan and West."

APPENDIX

MILLARD FILLMORE,

President of the United States of America,
To his Imperial Majesty,
THE EMPEROR OF JAPAN

Great and Good Friend!

I send you this public letter by Commodore Matthew C. Perry, an officer of highest rank in the Navy of the United States, and commander of the squadron now visiting your Imperial Majesty's dominions.

I have directed Commodore Perry to assure your Imperial Majesty that I entertain the kindest feelings toward your Majesty's person and government; and that I have no other object in sending him to Japan, but to propose to your Imperial Majesty that the United States and Japan should live in friendship, and have commercial intercourse with each other.

The constitution and laws of the United States forbid all interference with the religious or political concerns of other nations. I have particularly charged Commodore Perry to abstain from every act which could possibly disturb the tranquility of your Imperial Majesty's dominions.

The United States of America reach from ocean to ocean, and our territory of Oregon and state of California lie directly opposite to the dominions of your Imperial Majesty. Our steamships can go from California to Japan in eighteen days.

Our great state of California produces about sixty millions of dollars in gold, every year, besides silver, quicksilver, precious stones, and many other valuable articles. Japan is also a rich and fertile country, and produces many very valuable articles. Your Imperial Majesty's subjects are skilled in many of the arts. I am desirous that our two countries should trade with each other, for the benefit both of Japan and the United States.

We know that the ancient laws of your Imperial Majesty's government do not allow foreign trade except with the Dutch. But as the state of the world changes, and new governments are formed, it seems to be wise from time to time to make new laws. There was a time when the ancient laws of your Imperial Majesty's government were first made.

About the same time, America, which is sometimes called the New World, was first discovered and settled by the Europeans. For a long time there were but a few people, and they were poor. They have now become quite numerous; their commerce is very extensive; and they think that if your Imperial Majesty were so far to change ancient laws as to allow a free trade between the two countries, it would be extremely beneficial to both.

If your Imperial Majesty is not satisfied that it would be safe, altogether, to abrogate the ancient laws which forbid foreign trade, they might be suspended for five or ten years, so as to try the experiment. If it does not prove as beneficial as was hoped, the ancient laws can be restored. The United States often limit their treaties with foreign states to a few years, and then renew them or not, as they please.

I have directed Commodore Perry to mention another thing to your Imperial Majesty. Many of our ships pass every year from California to China; and great numbers of our people pursue the whale fishery near the shores of Japan. It sometimes happens in stormy weather that one of our ships is wrecked on your Imperial Majesty's shores. In all such cases we ask and expect, that our unfortunate people should be treated with kindness, and that their property should be protected, till we can send a vessel and bring them away. We are very much in earnest in this.

Commodore Perry is also directed by me to represent to your Imperial Majesty that we understand there is a great abundance of coal and provisions in the empire of Japan. Our steamships, in crossing the great ocean, burn a great deal of coal, and it is not convenient to bring it all the way from America. We wish that our steamships and other vessels should be allowed to stop in Japan and supply themselves with coal, provisions, and water. They will pay for them, in money, or anything else your Imperial Majesty's subjects may prefer; and we request your Imperial Majesty to appoint a convenient port in the southern part of the empire, where our vessels may stop for this purpose. We are very desirous of this.

These are the only objects for which I have sent Commodore Perry with a powerful squadron to pay a visit to your Imperial Majesty's renowned city of Yedo: friendship, commerce, a supply of coal, and provision and protection for our shipwrecked people.

We have directed Commodore Perry to beg your Imperial Majesty's acceptance of a few presents. They are of no great value in themselves, but some of them may serve as specimens of the articles manufactured in the United States, and they are intended as tokens of our sincere and respectful friendship.

May the Almighty have your Imperial Majesty in his great and holy keeping!

In witness whereof I have caused the great seal of the United States to be hereunto affixed, and have subscribed the same with my name, at the city of Washington in America, the seat of my government, on the thirteenth day of the month of November, in the year one thousand eight hundred and fifty-two.

Your Good Friend,
MILLARD FILLMORE.

By the President.
EDWARD EVERETT,
    Secretary of State.

CONVENTION BETWEEN THE UNITED
STATES OF AMERICA AND JAPAN,
SIGNED AT KANAGAWA, 31 MARCH 1874

The United States of America and the Empire of Japan, desiring to establish firm, lasting, and sincere friendship between the two nations, have resolved to fix, in a manner clear and positive, by means of a treaty or general convention of peace and amity, the rules which shall in future be mutually observed in the intercourse of their respective countries; for which most desirable object the President of the United States has conferred full powers on his commissioner, Matthew Calbraith Perry, special ambassador of the United States to Japan; and the august sovereign of Japan has given similar full powers to his commissioners, Hayashi-Daigaku-no-kami; Ido, Prince of Tsus-shima; Izawa, Prince of Mema-saki, and Udono, member of the Board of Revenue.

And the said commissioners, after having exchanged their said full powers, and duly considered the premises, have agreed to the following articles:

ARTICLE I

There shall be a perfect, permanent, and universal peace, and a sincere and cordial amity, between the United States of America on the one part, and the Empire of Japan on the other, and between their people, respectively, without exception of persons or places.

ARTICLE II

The port of Shimoda, in the principality of Izu, and the port of Hakodate, in the principality of Matsumai, are granted by the Japanese as ports for the reception of American ships, where they can be supplied with wood, water, provisions, and coal, and other articles their necessities may require, as far as the Japanese have them. The time for opening the first-named port is immediately on signing this treaty; the last-named port is to be opened immediately after the same day in the ensuing Japanese year.

NOTE. A tariff of prices shall be given by the Japanese officers of the things which they can furnish, payment for which shall be made in gold and silver coin.

ARTICLE III

Whenever ships of the United States are thrown or wrecked on the coast of Japan, the Japanese vessels will assist them, and carry their crews to Shimoda or Hakodate, and hand them over to their countrymen appointed to receive them. Whatever articles the shipwrecked men may have preserved shall likewise be restored, and the expenses incurred in the rescue and support of American and Japanese, who may thus be thrown upon the shores of either nation, are not to be refunded.

ARTICLE IV

Those shipwrecked persons and other citizens of the United States shall be free as in other countries, and not subjected to confinement, but shall be amenable to just laws.

ARTICLE V

Shipwrecked men, and other citizens of the United States, temporarily living at Shimoda and Hakodate, shall not be subject to such restrictions and confinement as the Dutch and Chinese are at Nagasaki; but shall be free at Shimoda to go where they please within the limits of seven Japanese miles (or *ri*) from a small island in the harbor of Shimoda, marked on the accompanying chart, hereto appended; and shall in like manner be free to go where they please at Hakodate, within limits to be defined after the visit of the United States squadron to that place.

ARTICLE VI

If there be any other sort of goods wanted, or any business which shall require to be arranged, there shall be careful deliberation between the parties in order to settle such matters.

ARTICLE VII

It is agreed that ships of the United States resorting to the ports open to them shall be permitted to exchange gold and silver coin, and articles of goods, for other articles of goods, under such regulations as shall be temporarily established by the Japanese government for that purpose. It is stipulated, however, that the ships of the United States shall be permitted to carry away whatever articles they are unwilling to exchange.

ARTICLE VIII

Wood, water, provisions, coal, and goods required shall only be procured through the agency of Japanese officers appointed for that purpose, and in no other manner.

ARTICLE IX

It is agreed, that if, at any future day, the government of Japan shall grant to any other nation or nations privileges and advantages which are not herein granted to the United States and the citizens thereof, that the same privileges and advantages shall be granted likewise to the United States and to the citizens thereof without any consultation or delay.

ARTICLE X

Ships of the United States shall be permitted to resort to no other ports in Japan but Shimoda and Hakodate, unless in distress or forced by stress of weather.

ARTICLE XI

There shall be appointed by the government of the United States consuls or agents to reside in Shimoda at any time after the expiration of eighteen months from the date of the signing of this treaty; provided that either of the two governments deems such arrangement necessary.

ARTICLE XII

The present convention, having been concluded and duly signed, shall be obligatory, and faithfully observed by the United States of America and Japan, and by the citizens and subjects of each respective power; and it is to be ratified and approved by the President of the United States, by and with the advice and consent of the Senate thereof, and by the august Sovereign of Japan, and the ratifications shall be exchanged within eighteen months from the date of the signature thereof, or sooner if practicable.

In faith whereof, we, the respective plenipotentiaries of the United States of America and the Empire of Japan, aforesaid, have signed and sealed these presents.

Done at Kanagawa, this thirty-first day of March, in the year of our Lord Jesus Christ one thousand eight hundred and fifty-four, and of Keyei the seventh year, third month, and third day.

TREATY BETWEEN THE UNITED STATES AND JAPAN, SIGNED ON 29 JULY 1858

The President of the United States of America and His Majesty the Ty-Coon of Japan, desiring to establish on firm and lasting foundations the relations of peace and friendship now happily existing between the two countries, and to secure the best interest of their respective citizens and subjects by encouraging, facilitating, and regulating their industry and trade, have resolved to conclude a Treaty of Amity and Commerce for this purpose, and have, therefore, named as their Plenipotentiaries, that is to say: the President of the United States, his Excellency Townsend Harris, Consul General of the United States of America for the Empire of Japan; and His Majesty the Ty-Coon of Japan, their Excellencies Ino-oo-ye, Prince of Sinano [Inouye Kiyonao, Shinano-no-kami], and Iwasay, Prince of Hego [Iwase Tadanari, Higo-no-kami]; who, after having communicated to each other their respective full powers, and found them to be in good and due form, have agreed upon and concluded the following Articles:

ARTICLE I

There shall henceforth be perpetual peace and friendship between the United States of America and His Majesty the Ty-Coon of Japan and his successors.

The President of the United States may appoint a Diplomatic Agent to reside at the city of Yedo, and Consuls or Consular Agents to reside at any or all of the ports in Japan which are opened for American commerce by this Treaty. The Diplomatic Agent and Consul General of the United States shall have the right to travel freely in any part of the Empire of Japan from the time they enter on the discharge of their official duties.

The Government of Japan may appoint a Diplomatic Agent to reside at Washington, and Consuls or Consular Agents for any or all of the ports of the United States. The Diplomatic Agent and Consul General of Japan may travel freely in any part of the United States from the time they arrive in the country.

ARTICLE II

The President of the United States, at the request of the Japanese Government, will act as a friendly mediator in such matters of difference as may arise between the Government of Japan and any European Power.

The ships-of-war of the United States shall render friendly aid and assistance to such Japanese vessels as they may meet on the high seas, so far as it can be done without a breach of neutrality; and all American Consuls residing at ports visited by Japanese vessels shall also give them such friendly aid as may be permitted by the laws of the respective countries in which they reside.

ARTICLE III

In addition to the ports of Simoda [Shimoda] and Hakodade [Hakodate], the following ports and towns shall be opened on the dates respectively appended to them, that is to say: Kanagawa, on the 4th of July, 1859; Nagasaki, on the 4th of July, 1859; Nee-e-gata [Niigata], on the 1st of January, 1860; Hiogo [Hyōgo], on the 1st of January, 1863.

If Nee-e-gata is found to be unsuitable as a harbor, another port on the west coast of Nipon shall be selected by the two Governments in lieu thereof. Six months after the opening of Kanagawa, the port of Simoda shall be closed as a place of residence and trade for American citizens. In all the foregoing ports and towns American citizens may permanently reside; they shall have the right to lease ground, and purchase the buildings thereon, and may erect dwellings and warehouses. But no fortification or place of military strength shall be erected under pretence of building dwellings or warehouses; and, to see that this Article is observed, the Japanese authorities shall have the right to inspect, from time to time, any buildings which are being erected, altered, or repaired. The place which the Americans shall occupy for their buildings, and the harbor regulations, shall be arranged by the American Consul and the authorities of each place, and, if they cannot agree, the matter shall be referred to and settled by the American Diplomatic Agent and the Japanese Government.

No wall, fence, or gate shall be erected by the Japanese around the place of residence of the Americans, or anything done which may prevent a free egress and ingress to the same.

From the 1st of January, 1862, Americans shall be allowed to reside in the city of Yedo; and from the 1st of January,

1863, in the city of Osaca [Ōsaka], for the purposes of trade only. In each of these two cities a suitable place within which they may hire houses, and the distance they may go, shall be arranged by the American Diplomatic Agent and the Government of Japan. Americans may freely buy from Japanese and sell to them any articles that either may have for sale, without the intervention of any Japanese officers in such purchase or sale, or in making or receiving payment for the same; and all classes of Japanese may purchase, sell, keep, or use any articles sold to them by the Americans.

The Japanese Government will cause this clause to be made public in every part of the Empire as soon as the ratifications of this Treaty shall be exchanged.

Munitions of war shall only be sold to the Japanese Government and foreigners.

No rice or wheat shall be exported from Japan as cargo, but all Americans resident in Japan, and ships, for their crews and passengers, shall be furnished with sufficient supplies of the same. The Japanese Government will sell, from time to time at public auction, any surplus quantity of copper that may be produced. Americans residing in Japan shall have the right to employ Japanese as servants or in any other capacity.

ARTICLE IV

Duties shall be paid to the Government of Japan on all goods landed in the country, and on all articles of Japanese production that are exported as cargo, according to the tariff hereunto appended.

If the Japanese Custom House officers are dissatisfied with the value placed on any goods by the owner, they may place a value thereon, and offer to take the goods at that valuation. If the owner refuses to accept the offer, he shall pay duty on such valuation. If the offer be accepted by the owner, the purchase-money shall be paid to him without delay, and without any abatement or discount.

Supplies for the use of the United States navy may be landed at Kanagawa, Hakodade, and Nagasaki, and stored in ware-houses, in the custody of an officer of the American Government, without the payment of any duty. But, if any such supplies are sold in Japan, the purchaser shall pay the proper duty to the Japanese authorities.

The importation of opium is prohibited; and, any American vessel coming to Japan for the purposes of trade having more than three catties (four pounds avoirdupois) weight of opium on board, such surplus quantity shall be seized and destroyed by the Japanese authorities. All goods imported into Japan, and which have paid the duty fixed by this Treaty, may be transported by the Japanese into any part of the empire without the payment of any tax, excise, or transit duty whatever.

No higher duties shall be paid by Americans on goods imported into Japan than are fixed by this Treaty, nor shall any higher duties be paid by Americans than are levied on the same description of goods if imported in Japanese vessels, or the vessels of any other nation.

ARTICLE V

All foreign coin shall be current in Japan and pass for its corresponding weight of Japanese coin of the same description. Americans and Japanese may freely use foreign or Japanese coin in making payments to each other.

As some time will elapse before the Japanese will be acquainted with the value of foreign coin, the Japanese Government will, for the period of one year after the opening of each harbor, furnish the Americans with Japanese coin in exchange for theirs, equal weights being given and no discount taken for re-coinage. Coins of all description (with the exception of Japanese copper coin) may be exported from Japan, and foreign gold and silver uncoined.

ARTICLE VI

Americans committing offences against Japanese shall be tried in American Consular courts, and, when guilty, shall be punished according to American law. Japanese committing offences against Americans shall be tried by the Japanese authorities and punished according to Japanese law. The Consular courts shall be open to Japanese creditors, to enable them to recover their just claims against American citizens; and the Japanese courts shall in like manner be open to American citizens for the recovery of their just claims against Japanese.

All claims for forfeitures or penalties for violations of this Treaty, or of the Articles regulating trade which are appended hereunto, shall be sued for in the Consular courts, and all recoveries shall be delivered to the Japanese authorities.

Neither the American or Japanese Governments are to be held responsible for the payment of any debts contracted by their respective citizens or subjects.

ARTICLE VII

In the opened harbors of Japan, Americans shall be free to go where they please, within the following limits:

At Kanagawa, the River Logo [Rokugo] (which empties into the Bay of Yedo between Kawasaki and Sinagawa), and 10 ri in any other direction.

At Hakodade, 10 ri in any direction.

At Hiogo, 10 ri in any direction, that of Kioto [Kyōto] excepted, which city shall not be approached nearer than 10 ri. The crews of vessels resorting to Hiogo shall not cross the River Enagawa, which empties into the Bay between Hiogo and Osaca. The distance shall be measured inland from Goyoso [Goyōsho], or town hall of each of the foregoing harbors, the ri being equal to 4,275 yards American measure.

At Nagasaki, Americans may go into any part of the Imperial domain in its vicinity. The boundaries of Nee-e-gata, or the place that may be substituted for it, shall be settled by the American Diplomatic Agent and the Government of Japan. Americans who have been convicted of felony, or twice convicted of misdemeanors, shall not go more than one Japanese ri inland from the places of their respective residences, and all persons so convicted shall lose their right of permanent residence in Japan, and the Japanese authorities may require them to leave the country.

A reasonable time shall be allowed to all such persons to settle their affairs, and the American Consular authority shall, after an examination into the circumstances of each case, determine the time to be allowed, but such time shall not in any case exceed one year, to be calculated from the time the person shall be free to attend to his affairs.

ARTICLE VIII

Americans in Japan shall be allowed the free exercise of their religion, and for this purpose shall have the right to erect suitable places of worship. No injury shall be done to such buildings, nor any insult be offered to the religious worship of the Americans. American citizens shall not injure any Japanese temple or *mia* [*miya*], or offer any insult or injury to Japanese religious ceremonies or to the objects of their worship.

The Americans and Japanese shall not do anything that may be calculated to excite religious animosity. The Government of Japan has already abolished the practice of trampling on religious emblems.

ARTICLE IX

When requested by the American Consul, the Japanese authorities will cause the arrest of all deserters and fugitives from justice, receive in jail all persons held as prisoners by the Consul, and give to the Consul such assistance as may be required to enable him to enforce the observance of the laws by the Americans who are on land, and to maintain order among the shipping. For all such service, and for the support of prisoners kept in confinement, the Consul shall in all cases pay a just compensation.

ARTICLE X

The Japanese Government may purchase or construct in the United States ships-of-war, steamers, merchant ships, whale ships, cannon, munitions of war, and arms of all kinds, and any other things it may require. It shall have the right to engage in the United States scientific, naval and military men, artisans of all kinds, and mariners to enter into its service. All purchases made for the Government of Japan may be exported from the United States, and all persons engaged for its service may freely depart from the United States: provided that no articles that are contraband of war shall be exported, nor any persons engaged to act in a naval or military capacity, while Japan shall be at war with any Power in amity with the United States.

ARTICLE XI

The Articles for the regulation of trade, which are appended to this Treaty, shall be considered as forming a part of the same, and shall be equally binding on both the Contracting Parties to this Treaty, and on their citizens and subjects.

ARTICLE XII

Such of the provisions of the Treaty made by Commodore Perry, and signed at Kanagawa, on the 31st of March 1854, as conflict with the provisions of this Treaty are hereby revoked; and, as all the provisions of a Convention executed by the Consul General of the United States and the Governors of Simoda, on the 17th of June, 1857, are incorporated in this Treaty, that Convention is also revoked.

The person charged with the diplomatic relations of the United States in Japan, in conjunction with such person or persons as may be appointed for that purpose by the Japanese Government, shall have power to make such rules and regulations as may be required to carry into full and complete effect the provisions of this Treaty, and the provisions of the Articles regulating trade appended thereunto.

ARTICLE XIII

After the 4th of July, 1872, upon the desire of either the American or Japanese Governments, and one year's notice given by either party, this Treaty, and such portions of the Treaty of Kanagawa as remain unrevoked by this Treaty, together with the regulations of trade hereunto annexed, or those that may be hereafter introduced, shall be subject to revision by Commissioners appointed on both sides for this purpose, who will be empowered to decide on, and insert therein, such amendments as experience shall prove to be desirable.

ARTICLE XIV

This Treaty shall go into effect on the 4th of July, 1859, on or before which day the ratifications of the same shall be exchanged at the City of Washington; but if, from any unforeseen cause, the ratifications cannot be exchanged by that time, the Treaty shall still go into effect at the date above mentioned.

The act of ratification on the part of the United States shall be verified by the signature of the President of the United States, countersigned by the Secretary of State, and sealed with the seal of the United States.

The act of ratification on the part of Japan shall be verified by the name and seal of His Majesty the Ty-Coon, and by the seals and signatures of such of his high officers as he may direct.

This Treaty is executed in quadruplicate, each copy being written in the English, Japanese, and Dutch languages, all the versions having the same meaning and intention, but the Dutch version shall be considered as being the original.

In witness whereof, the above-named Plenipotentiaries have hereunto set their hands and seals, at the City of Yedo, this 29th day of July, in the year of Our Lord 1858, and of the Independence of the United States of America the eighty-third, corresponding to the Japanese era, the 19th day of the sixth month of the 5th year of Ansei, *Mma*.

SOURCES AND NOTES

The works from which selections have been quoted are listed below; their titles are abbreviated in the Notes that follow. Numbers at the left in the Notes represent pages in this edition on which specific selections appear.

[HARRIS, TOWNSEND.] *The Complete Journal of Townsend Harris,* introduction and notes by Mario E. Cosenza. Published for Japan Society, New York; Garden City, New York, Doubleday, Doran and Co., 1930.

[HAYASHI, NOBORU.] *Diary of an Official of the Bakufu,* translated by E. W. Clements. Transactions of the Asiatic Society of Japan, Second Series, Vol. VII; London, Kegan Paul, Trench, Trubner & Co., 1930.

[HECO, JOSEPH.] *Narrative of a Japanese,* edited by James Murdoch. Yokohama, Yokohama Printing and Publishing Co., n.d. (2 vols.; all quotations from Vol. 1)

KAEMPFER, ENGELBERT. *The History of Japan,* translated by J. G. Scheuchzer. Printed for the translator, London, 1727; also Glasgow, James MacLehose & Sons, 1906. (3 vols.; all quotations from Vol. 1)

KING, C. W. *Notes of the Voyage of the Morrison from Canton to Japan,* Vol. 1 of *Claims of Japan and Malaysia upon Christendom.* New York, E. French, 1839.

Ranald MacDonald, edited by William S. Lewis and Naojiro Murakami. Spokane, Wash., Eastern Washington State Historical Society, 1923.

Manners and Customs of the Japanese in the Nineteenth Century. New York, Harper and Brothers, 1841.

Narrative of the Expedition of an American Naval Squadron to the China Seas and Japan, compiled by Francis L. Hawks. Published by order of the Congress of the United States, Washington, D.C., 1856. (3 vols.; all quotations from Vol. 1)

The New York Daily Times (dates as given; abbreviated as *Times*)

NITOBE, INAZO. *The Japanese Nation, Its Land, Its People and Its Life.* New York, G. P. Putnam's Sons, 3rd printing, 1912.

PAINE, RALPH D. *Ships and Sailors of Old Salem.* New York, Outing Publishing Co., 1908.

[PERRY, MATTHEW C.] *The Personal Journal of Commodore Matthew C. Perry,* edited by Roger Pineau. Washington, D.C., Smithsonian Institution Press, 1968.

Select Documents on Japanese Foreign Policy, 1853–1868, translated and edited by W. G. Beasley. London and New York, Oxford University Press, 1955.

Sources of Japanese Tradition, compiled by Ryusaku Tsunoda, William Theodore DeBary, Donald Keene. New York, Columbia University Press, 1958; paperback edn., in 2 vols., 1964 (All quotations from Vol. 2 of the paper edn.)

SPALDING, J. W. *The Japan Expedition.* Redfield, New York, 1855.

TANABE, MORIYUKE. Letter to Gretchen Amussen, April 13, 1969.

TAYLOR, BAYARD. *A Visit to India, China and Japan, 1853.* New York, G. P. Putnam's Sons, 1870.

THUNBERG, KARL PETER. *Travels in Europe, Africa and Asia, 1770–1779.* Printed for F. & C. Rivington, London, 1796. (4 vols.; all quotations from Vol. 4)

NOTES

6   Spalding, pp. 234–35

7   Kaempfer, bk. 4, p. 325

7   *Manners and Customs,* p. 97

7   *Ibid.,* p. 99

8   Thunberg, p. 11

20–22   Paine, pp. 334–36 (paraphrased)

25   *Ibid.,* pp. 373–74

26, 28   *Ibid.,* pp. 339–40

30–31   *Sources of Japanese Tradition,* pp. 88–90

31–32   *Ibid.,* p. 94

34   King, p. 135

36   Nitobe, pp. 269–70

37   *Ibid.,* pp. 268–69

38–39   *MacDonald,* p. 271

39   *Ibid.,* p. 272

40–41   *Ibid.,* pp. 276–77

41   *Ibid.,* p. 279

43–44   *Ibid.,* p. 280

45   *Ibid.,* p. 275

45   *Ibid.,* p. 271

47　Heco, p. 3
47–48　*Ibid.*, pp. 33–34
53–54　*Ibid.*, p. 89
55　*Ibid.*, p. 115
62–63　*Times,* Feb. 2, 1852
63　*Narrative of the Expedition,*
　　p. 76
63　*Times,* Feb. 2, 1852
64　*Ibid.*
64　*Ibid.*, Feb. 24, 1852
64–65　*Ibid.*
65　*Ibid.*, June 15, 1852
66, 69　*Narrative of the Expedi-*
　　tion, p. 77
70, 72　*Times,* Jan. 31, 1853
72　Taylor, p. 358
72　*Ibid.*, p. 361
73　*Narrative of the Expedition,*
　　p. 228
81　*Ibid.*, p. 235
85　*Ibid.*, p. 238
88–89　*Ibid.*, p. 244
89　*Ibid.*, pp. 245–46
89–90　*Ibid.*, p. 247
90　*Ibid.*, p. 248
92　*Ibid.* p. 253
92　*Ibid.*
95　*Ibid.*, p. 255
97–98　*Ibid.*, pp. 260–61
98　*Ibid.*, p. 261
99　*Ibid.*, p. 263
103, 106–10　*Select Documents,*
　　pp. 114–17
110–12　*Ibid.*, pp. 112–14
112–17　*Ibid.*, pp. 117–19
121　Perry, *Journal,* p. 156
121　Spalding, p. 213
121　*Ibid.*, p. 213–14
123　Perry, *Journal,* p. 158
123　*Narrative of the Expedi-*
　　tion, p. 331

123–24　Hayashi, p. 98
124　*Narrative of the Expedi-*
　　tion, pp. 331–32
124–25　*Ibid.*, pp. 332–33
125　*Ibid.*, p. 333
125　Hayashi, p. 99
125–26　*Narrative of the Expe-*
　　dition, p. 335
126　Perry, *Journal,* p. 161
127　Hayashi, p. 100
127　*Ibid.*, pp. 100–01
127–28　*Narrative of the Expe-*
　　dition, p. 338
128　Spalding, p. 220
128　*Ibid.*
128–29　*Ibid.*, p. 221
130　Hayashi, p. 101
130　*Ibid.*
135–36　*Narrative of the Expe-*
　　dition, pp. 349–50
137–44　Hayashi, pp. 102–06
147–48　*Ibid.*, p. 107
149　*Narrative of the Expedi-*
　　tion, p. 369
149　*Ibid.*, p. 370
149　Hayashi, pp. 111–12
153　*Narrative of the Expedi-*
　　tion, p. 371
153　*Ibid.*, p. 375
154　Hayashi, p. 112
154　Spalding, p. 250
154　*Narrative of the Expedi-*
　　tion, p. 376
154　Hayashi, p. 112
154–55　*Ibid.*, p. 113
155　*Ibid.*
155–56　*Ibid.*
156　*Ibid.*, p. 114
156　*Ibid.*, p. 115
157　*Ibid.*, p. 117
157–58　*Ibid.*, p. 117–18

158 *Narrative of the Expedition*, pp. 396–97
160 *Ibid.*, p. 398
160 *Ibid.*, p. 399
161–62 Hayashi, pp. 118–19
162–68, 170 *Select Documents*, pp. 122–27
171–72 *Times*, June 13, 1854
172 Perry, *Journal*, p. 176
172–73 *Narrative of the Expedition*, pp. 387–90
177 Harris, *Journal*, p. 9
177 *Ibid.*, pp. 27–28
178 *Ibid.*, p. 195
179 *Ibid.*, p. 196
179 *Ibid.*, p. 199
181 *Ibid.*, p. 208
181 *Ibid.*, p. 205
182 *Ibid.*, p. 210
183 *Ibid.*, p. 217
184 *Ibid.*, p. 225
186 *Ibid.*, pp. 231–32
186 *Ibid.*, p. 246
186–87 *Ibid.*, p. 247
187 *Ibid.*, p. 252
187 *Ibid.*, p. 240
188 *Ibid.*, p. 254
188 *Ibid.*, p. 256
188–89 *Ibid.*, p. 293
189 *Ibid.*, pp. 296–97
189 *Ibid.*, p. 301
193 *Ibid.*, pp. 357–58
193 *Ibid.*, p. 366
194 *Ibid.*, p. 378
196 *Ibid.*, p. 406

198 *Ibid.*, pp. 428–29
199–200 *Ibid.*, pp. 436–37
201 *Ibid.*, p. 444
202 *Ibid.*, p. 475
202 *Ibid.*
203–04 *Ibid.*, p. 486
204 *Ibid.*
204–05 *Select Documents*, p. 162
205 *Ibid.*, p. 163
205 *Ibid.*, pp. 163–64
205 *Ibid.*, p. 164
205 *Ibid.*, pp. 164–65
208 Harris, *Journal*, p. 497
208 *Select Documents*, p. 165
208 *Ibid.*, p. 166
208–09 *Ibid.*, pp. 166–68
210 *Ibid.*, p. 169
210 *Ibid.*, p. 177
210–13 *Ibid.*, pp. 179–80
213 Harris, *Journal*, p. 496
214 *Ibid.*, p. 497
214–15 *Ibid.*, p. 500
215 *Ibid.*, p. 505
217 *Ibid.*, p. 518
217 *Ibid.*, p. 517
217 *Ibid.*, p. 518
218 *Ibid.*, p. 539
220–22 *Select Documents*, pp. 180–81
223–27 *Ibid.*, pp. 189–93
228–29 *Ibid.*, pp. 193–94
235 Moriyuki Tanabe
242–50 *Select Documents*, pp. 183–89

FOR FURTHER READING

BEASLEY, W. G. *The Modern History of Japan.* New York, 1963.

HALL, JOHN W. and BEARDSLEY, RICHARD K. *Twelve Doors to Japan.* New York, 1965.

MORISON, SAMUEL. *Old Bruin: Commodore Matthew C. Perry, 1794–1858.* Boston, 1967.

———. *Maritime History of Massachusetts, 1783–1860.* Paperback edn., Boston, 1961.

MURDOCH, JAMES. *A History of Japan.* Kobe, 1910.

REISCHAUER, EDWIN O. *The United States and Japan.* 3d edn., Cambridge, Mass., 1965; paperback edn., New York, 1962.

———, and Fairbank, John K. *East Asia: The Great Tradition* (Vol. 1 of *History of East Asian Civilization*). Boston, 1960.

REYNOLDS, ROBERT L. *Perry in Japan.* New York, 1963.

SANSOM, GEORGE B. *History of Japan* (3 vols.; 1: to 1334; 2: 1334–1615; 3:1615–1867). Stanford, Calif., 1958, 1961, and 1963 respectively.

———. *The Western World and Japan.* New York, 1950.

SMITH, BRADLEY. *Japan: A History in Art.* New York, 1964.

WALWORTH, ARTHUR. *Black Ships Off Japan.* New York, 1946.

WARRINER, EMILY V. *Voyager to Destiny.* Indianapolis, 1956.

INDEX